# A PLATE FULL OF

"April Kelly serves up a buffet of luscious recipes for online star-studded success. Dish it out!"

**Cynthia Brian, New York Times best-selling author**
**TV/Radio personality/ Founder,**
**Be the Star You Are!° charity**

"This truly is networking advice that sticks!"

**Janet Bray Attwood, New York Times Bestseller**
*The Passion Test: The Effortless Path to Living Your Life Purpose*

"I have worked with April on many occasions and have always been impressed with her knowledge, her passion, and her vision. And with *Spaghetti on the Wall* she hits it out of the park once again. In this digital age we are bombarded with images and impressions. To be able to stand out, be noticed and be remembered these days is more difficult than ever. April gives some good, insightful approaches to branding and networking yourself in this changing environment. With ideas like these I can't wait to work with her again soon. It's a great read. Get *Spaghetti on the Wall*."

**Tom Becka, Award-Winning Author**
**Morning Radio Personality, 101.9 Talk FM, Fargo**
*There's No Business Without the Show:*
*Using Show Biz Skills to get Blockbuster Sales!*

"As one of the early executives at both PayPal and LinkedIn, April Kelly had a front-row view of the social media revolution. Now she brings that wealth of experience to everyone in an easy-to-digest, immediately actionable book that will help you build a winning brand. Following April's advice will change your career."

**Jeff Beals, Award-Winning Author**
*Self Marketing Power: Branding Yourself as a Business of One*

"April Kelly's *Spaghetti on the Wall* is the Rosetta Stone for social networks. April defines and differentiates them and makes them understandable. April Kelly's book is the GPS that will then navigate you to get to where you want to go. She maximizes this tool for your career. April Kelly's book helps you market YOU. She takes you step by step up your goal ladder via social networks in your best possible light. *Spaghetti on the Wall* is like having a personal consultant for your career in the 21$^{st}$ Century."

**JJ Kennedy, Radio Personality**
**Talk WOR-A, New York**

"In today's economy personal and professional branding is critical to successfully gaining employment or advancing in the workplace. *Spaghetti on the Wall* a must read for anyone who wants to leave a positive and memorable impact on those they encounter. April Kelly will soon become a household name for everyone wishing to stand out from the crowd. Kelly gives you the recipe and all the ingredients you need to brand yourself and become just as "sticky" as *Spaghetti on the Wall*."

**Sheilah Etheridge, SME Management**
**LinkedIn Power User**

BRANDING &
NETWORKING
METHODS THAT
STICK!

# Spaghetti
## on
### the wall

BRANDING & NETWORKING METHODS THAT STICK!

Spaghetti on the wall

# APRIL KELLY
Social Marketing Trailblazer

WOOHOO
PRESS, LLC

Omaha, Nebraska

ISBN13: 978-0-9824386-2-6
Library of Congress Control Number: 2012901495

Woohoo Press, LLC
Gretna, NE
www.AuthorAprilKelly.com

Cover Design © TLC Graphics, www.TLCGraphics.com
Book Design, Production and Marketing: Concierge Marketing, Inc.
Printed in the United States
10 9 8 7 6 5 4 3 2 1

To my parents,
for planting my roots deep and supporting my adventure.


To my brother Steve,
for his never-ending prayerful guidance.


To my children,
for keeping it light and keeping my feet on the ground.

# Contents

# Foreword:
# David G. Thomson

**W**hat do Facebook, Twitter, LinkedIn, and your visibility to others have in common globally? *Exponential growth.* You have the power to leverage connections and relationships to grow a personal network at an astounding growth rate. You must manage your brand and network to achieve your goals as a prerequisite to navigating these uncertain times.

Managing your network and your brand is now a full-blown science. *Spaghetti on the Wall* is your blueprint to create *the Power of Me.*

What you do with the people you know and how you influence others is the difference-making trait found among the most successful and happiest people. This can be you.

More than just an overview of online networking, *Spaghetti on the Wall* applies the science of networking and personal branding to provide the tools that a highly motivated person—like you—can apply to create huge impact for yourself and others.

I have had the privilege of knowing April Kelly for many years when she served as the Senior Director of Operations at LinkedIn. I was inspired that she created and led a team in Omaha that served LinkedIn customers worldwide.

April has done an outstanding job of describing personal networking and branding that works and why it works. She has analyzed the winning approaches that can work for you to achieve your goals. April unlocks the secrets so you can apply an integrated approach to becoming a leader in personal networking and branding.

The real value of April's book is not what she writes. It is what you do with what you learn. Follow in the footsteps of this master.

David G. Thomson

*David G. Thomson is a world-renowned business growth consultant, keynote speaker, and best-selling author. Thomson's books,* Blueprint to a Billion *and* 7 Essentials of High-Growth Companies *have been translated worldwide and featured in top media globally.*

# Acknowledgments

**W**riting this book has been a perfect exercise in branding and networking. I have had many people near and dear to me helping me through the process. I met most of these people through friends and an inquisitive spirit. I want to thank everyone whom I have had the honor of working with. I especially want to thank Sarah and her relentless spirit to win. She showed me the depths of courage and what it meant to "stretch."

I also want to thank my Omaha teams. You know who you are. You are the movers and shakers—the change makers. It was miraculous to watch you grow and serve. I consider it an honor to remain your friend and mentor in some cases.

I also want to thank the team working on this book: Lisa, Erin, Sandra, Jessica, and Ellie. Your humor and patience gave me a safe haven to launch another publication. I admire your patience, persistence, creativity, and vocabulary. Thank you.

I look forward to what the next steps will be and whom I will make them alongside. Life is truly about doing the right thing, helping others succeed, and paying forward. Branding and networking can help you and others get to where you want to be. Pass the Spaghetti.

# Introduction: Recipe for Success

**T**wo major buzz words in the business world right now are networking and branding. A lot of books will tell you how to do one or the other, although it is less common to unite the two. But *networking* and *branding* are two concepts that should go together.

Let's consider for a moment how the two are connected. Branding is essentially making yourself memorable in the corporate marketplace today. The largest employers receive hundreds, if not thousands, of résumés every month—even if they don't have any positions open! How do you set yourself apart from the thousands of other job seekers? Through personal branding.

Better yet, what if you are ready for a career change? How can you make the leap and establish yourself as a subject-matter expert in a new area? Branding is your key.

Networking, on the other hand, operates on the concept of "who you know." It's easier to get a job if you know someone in your field who can get you a position. Why does networking get you that job so much more easily? Because the person you know already has a concept of who you are, and he or she thinks well of you. In essence, this person already understands what you are about—your personal brand—even if you don't consciously have one in place. We all have our personal brands, whether we consciously create our brand or not, and networking allows you to position yourself based on who you know—the "who" that already understands your personal brand.

You may not realize it, but you have a personal brand. The key to personal branding is consciously being able to control that brand, use it to your advantage, and actually make yourself stand out above all others in ways that rely less on knowing someone and more on the validity of yourself as a person and as the best candidate for any job you have your sights set on.

So does this mean that you don't need a network if you've got your personal branding in line? Certainly not! Your network and your personal brand should go hand in hand. Just remember that your personal brand is significantly weaker if it only stands on the shoulders of your network.

# NETWORKING

So networking is about who you know, but today's networks are significantly more complicated than networks of the past.

The term *networking* was brought into popular use when Amway coined the phrase "network marketing." In its simplest terms, the concept meant "people telling people," as opposed to people learning about a product or service from a vast advertising campaign.

Networking caught on famously, mainly because it gave individuals a sense of empowerment. The thinking became: *We can do this without mega advertising budgets. We'll just tell our friends and neighbors and coworkers and do the job ourselves.*

The more you network, the more people you have the opportunity to contact. But as you're networking, what are people telling others about you? Is that message consistent? This is where personal branding comes into the equation. If you have successfully branded yourself, then your network will deliver that message about you with ease to others.

In the corporate world, the connotation of networking leaned more toward who you knew. It equated to a thick stack of business cards and a bulging Rolodex. It was who invited you to lunch, and whom you invited to lunch, and the people you hung out with at the company party or after the company trade show.

This latter type of networking wasn't always the choice of the individual, but rather what was best for the company.

This is because few thought in terms of individuality, but each person was attempting to be the perfect *company* man or woman.

You come into contact with so many people each day that it's simply impossible to remember everyone. Even if someone else has made an impression on you, it doesn't mean that you've made an impression in return. The only way to truly build those network connections is to put some time and effort into them. This is the new way to network. You can really only count someone in your network if you actually know the person. Having someone's business card in your Rolodex doesn't count anymore.

## THE EVOLUTION OF NETWORKING

After the dawn of the new millennium, after the dot.com bust, after the onslaught of the popularity of blogging and the rise of social media marketing and Web 2.0, the networking landscape changed greatly.

Networking has now evolved into a full-blown science (or perhaps an art form, whichever perspective you may take). The scope of networking with the use of modern technology is nothing less than mind boggling—for many reasons, not the least of which is instant access via tools such as Facebook and LinkedIn to other individuals around the globe. Add to that the endless variety of online tools and techniques such as Twitter and blogging also available to achieve quality and effective connections and communication.

The new networking is an exciting concept for many. And those who have embraced it are benefitting in ways that colleagues just one generation before could never have imagined. Not in their wildest dreams.

The biggest issue with networking today in the environment of Web 2.0 is the transition from the Rolodex to the Facebook or LinkedIn page. Just because you have somebody's business card in your virtual or physical "Rolodex" doesn't mean he or she is in your network. Just "friending" someone on Facebook doesn't put the new contact in your network.

Sorry, folks. The Rolodex rule applies. If you don't actually know the person, then he or she is *not* in your network.

Unfortunately you may not be as far along in your network building efforts than you think you are. Having 983 "friends" or 1,233 "connections" does not a network make. Nonetheless, it is easy to get excited by all the connections you're able to make through social networking. And the good news is that once you have these connections online, it just takes a little more effort on your part to take those connections to the next level and start bringing them into your real network.

## Terrifying

Just as this new form of networking is exciting for some, it is also terrifying for others—namely, the Baby Boomer generation. Suddenly the game has changed. The rules you followed years ago when you first stepped into corporate America are completely different. Instead of just trying to be a dedicated company man or company woman, you're looking for more personal connections, and instead of just doling out as many business cards as you can, suddenly you've got to make more of an effort to interact with those you want to connect with. But what may be most terrifying of all for some Baby Boomers, and even for some Gen Xers, is dealing with all this new technology as part of your networking strategy.

A recent study out of the Pew Research Center tracked Baby Boomers' use of social networking sites such as LinkedIn and Facebook in 2009 and showed that the generation moving toward retirement is the fastest growing group on these sites, which makes sense because younger generations were already using them. But how many Baby Boomers know how to use these social networking sites to actually network in a way that benefits them and their career? Not many. Yet.

Of course, Baby Boomers shouldn't feel alone in this respect. Even the younger generations seem to be just as confused about how to use these social networking sites to their benefit. Sites like Facebook and especially LinkedIn are more than just a way to get back in touch with old high school friends or stay in contact with new ones.

These sites can either make or break your career—depending on how you use them. Like it or not, everything you do online is seen and can be monitored by others, including potential employers. If you're worried about your past coming back to haunt you, this is one way that "Me after the Prom" party pics or you with a Sharpie-made mustache passed out in the back seat of your questionable best buddy's car certainly can. However, you can avoid some major pitfalls by following the tips in this book.

## Overwhelming

Through social media and the Internet, you have the opportunity to touch just about anyone—even people who are halfway around the world! This thought alone can seem overwhelming, and the realization that you haven't been using every aspect of social networking to your full advantage doesn't help either.

So where do you start building your network? What are you supposed to do? It's no wonder most of us get so overwhelmed just by the mere thought of networking.

But anyone has the ability to use these tools to their full advantage. You just have to know where to begin, and this book will point you in the right direction. You'll get a clear path showing how to network in the way that will work best for you, for your particular needs and your particular situation. You'll also learn how personal branding is one of the keys that can help unlock the power of your personal network.

## PERSONAL BRANDING

What exactly is personal branding? When thinking of brands and branding, former generations conjured up such images as the red Coca Cola logo, the Golden Arches of McDonald's, Lacoste's crocodile, and the three-point Mercedes logo. These brands are recognizable anywhere. And immediately in your mind you can add dozens of others—many of which you've known from earliest childhood.

With regard to individuals, those in the media (entertainment and the arts) learned to hire professional public relations experts who could create their *persona*. The goal was to make that individual stand out in the crowd and be recognized and noticed. It was seldom referred to as *branding*, but the image-making amounted to the same thing. It was a sales job in the purest sense, and it came with an exorbitant price tag.

Branding, in today's vocabulary, is different, and it is vital that you learn what it means and how it affects you and your future.

In days past, if you had in hand a well-put-together résumé with a personalized and targeted cover letter, you were well equipped to launch your career. You were even more equipped if you actually had connections in some way to someone within the company to which you were applying.

Time to wake up and smell the double-shot espresso hold the sugar, because those days are over. There are almost 7 billion people in the world today, and if you're in a large city, you're up against hundreds of thousands of other individuals. How do you stand out from the crowd? The only way you can is through personal branding, a concept that hasn't been in the forefront of the corporate world for very long.

In August 1997, leadership guru and visionary named Tom Peters wrote an article entitled "The Brand Called You," which appeared in the magazine *Fast Company*. This article thrust the idea of personal, individualized branding onto center stage (consider yourself the CEO of Me, Inc.).

Peters said, "Regardless of age, regardless of position, regardless of the business we happen to be in, all of us need to understand the importance of branding. We are CEOs of our own companies: Me, Inc. To be in business today, our most important job is to be head marketer for the brand called You."

Since the birth of this idea, tools have evolved to support this theory and the concept has snowballed.

# THE POWER OF ME

It concerns me that so many newcomers into the workforce are not grasping the full meaning of personal branding and the power with which it can propel them into the top of their chosen field. And what is even more problematic is that many actually see the need to change the way they manage their career, but for various reasons they fail to accomplish that task. In this case, ignorance is not bliss. Failing to tap into this power can have devastating career results.

In a nutshell, personal branding means that even individuals employed within large companies are able to customize their own image, showcase their talents and abilities, and manage their own careers via personal branding.

Realize that in today's job market millions of résumés are stacking up on sites such as Monster.com, CareerBuilder.com, and HotJobs.com. Even if your résumé is the *best of the best*, how will you ever get the attention you deserve? Your résumé may show your achievements and education, but can it shine light on your personality?

And if you are stuck in a going-nowhere job, how can you begin to create your own persona that will give you a leg up to the job you really want?

Make success happen through personal and professional branding.

Why do you think headhunters pick and choose certain people for a particular job, even if that person has not applied for the position? It is possible to be tapped for a major position without even putting yourself out there with the aim of getting that position. Granted, this may be the exception rather than the norm, but what makes these people stand out is their personal branding. If you want to be sought after, you've got to stand out from the crowd and be memorable. Personal branding is the answer.

Keep in mind that recruiters now rely more and more on social media and networks. This practice will only increase in coming years. When it does, where will you be? What can you do today to ensure that you take full advantage of the seismic changes taking place? The answer is simple. Figure out your brand and then just put it out there so that it will be found.

## COMBINING NETWORKING AND PERSONAL BRANDING

The two concepts could be worlds apart, but networking and branding have more in common than you think. Both are important techniques to get your name out front in the business world, but the similarity does not stop there. Being successful at both of these techniques requires that you learn how to blend the two together and make them play off each other. You can start by thinking of your network as a vehicle through which your personal brand can and should be expressed.

Both networking and personal branding can only take you so far before each begins to need the other. Some people may consider themselves to be excellent networkers but not so good at this branding stuff. On the other hand, maybe you'll find out that branding is your strong suit, while networking is difficult. Whichever the case, the way to be successful is to combine the two. Make them both part of your personal marketing campaign.

Think for a moment about how companies create their advertising and marketing campaigns. Their advertisements must deliver their marketing and branding messages consistently. Those advertisements then create a network of customers who know and trust their product. Brand consistency leads to a larger network because more people recognize the product and where it came from.

Put the same principle to work for you. You'll use your personal branding message to establish who you are, and your network will help to circulate that message. Who better to promote your brand than the people who already know you?

*Spaghetti on the Wall* is designed to be your guide through the maze of how to effectively use online networking (and other methods) to enhance and define your personal brand. I trust that once you follow through the steps outlined here, you will be well on your way to discovering for yourself the amazing benefits of professional, personal branding. And in the process it will change your future for the better.

## Part One

Whetting Your Appetite for a
More Fulfilling Personal Brand

# 1. The Value of Networking

If someone sat you down at a table where in front of you lay a black velvet cloth strewn with loose uncut diamonds, could you tell which ones were the most valuable? What if you were given a strong magnifying glass? Could you then pick out which ones would be of the greatest value and which would be of lesser value?

The answer for most people is probably a vehement *no*. It's not because you lack intelligence, but you simply lack training in the value of uncut diamonds.

In that light, how would you measure the value of a social/business networking system? Let's go a little deeper. How would you personally measure the value of *your* current, in-place networking system? And has it been carefully and meticulously honed and cultivated? Or has it been left to chance? Perhaps you imagine a valuable stone will eventually evolve out of your mountain of data.

The difference between the two boils down to your grasp of the value of networking. If you've never been taught and trained how crucial networking is (and will continue to be) in the growth of your career, chances are you will trust it to grow on its own, like an uncut gemstone sitting in a pile of rocks. But the problem is that, just like a stone garden, no network can grow without some time and effort.

## YOUR NETWORK'S VALUE

Let's take a minute now and determine the value of your network. Think about all of the people you know, including those you have connected with via Facebook and LinkedIn. Chances are, you don't even know the names of these people without logging into your account and looking at your friends list. These are the people you can touch easily whenever you want to. You have the ability to forge deeper relationships with these people whenever you wish. If there's a mutual exchange that can happen between you, then it's a good idea to make that connection deeper than both of you just showing up on each other's friends list.

Now stop for a moment and think about the people you could actually call on if you're in a jam, such as being let go from a job. Suddenly your list is about five sizes smaller isn't it? If you don't have anyone in this last category, then the value of your network is quite small. Today's networks are about quality—not quantity. This is why some people are finding themselves trying to re-measure the value of their networks in this new way. Networking is no longer about how many people you know—at least not in the simplest sense. It's about how many meaningful connections you have.

Consider now the last time someone from your past suddenly called you out of the blue. You got the distinct impression she was only calling to ask you for a favor. This tends to be a turnoff for a fleeting call from someone you haven't heard from in a long time. The best way to avoid being in the caller's shoes is to nurture the important connections in your network. It's true that you won't have time to get to know everyone you've met very well, but you do have time to get to know a few people so well that you can call them if you're in a jam or if you have a friend who's in a jam.

## THE VALUE OF YOUR COMMODITY

Imagine for a moment that your network can be compared to a highly valued commodity such as gold. If that were so, would you manage your network any differently than you do now? Would you place a different value on it than you do now? And would you spend quality time to develop that network, knowing that you would be increasing the worth of your commodity?

The answer to most of these rhetorical questions would probably be yes! You wouldn't just throw your dollars out there and hope they land in a profitable place, just as you shouldn't toss your business cards out there and hope they land in the hands of someone who would be a good connection for you.

It's up to you to make those connections work, just as it's up to you to make smart investments so your dollars work for you. When you have a network that's very valuable, it's easy to make it work, both for you and for the other people who are in your network.

## YOUR GOODWILL AMBASSADORS

Let's use yet another analogy. Imagine your network as your goodwill ambassadors going out to pave the way for you—speaking a good word about you and showcasing your talents, abilities, and strengths.

Actually your network (or lack of the same) is out there working for you as a spokesperson of one sort or another. Again, stop and consider what is being related about you via your network.

If you have left your network totally to chance, then the message the world receives about you may come through fuzzy and garbled. Or worse, it may not come through at all. Conversations about you may go something like this:

"Jane Smith has you down as a reference. What's she like?"

"I haven't spoken to her in a while, but ten years ago she was a good worker."

Is that how you want your network to talk about you? No. Better yet, you want your network to say this:

"Jane Smith has you down as a reference. What's she like?"

"I had lunch with her just last month. She's a real go-getter. Let me tell you about some of her current projects."

These conversations can play out in many similar ways, depending on how well you know the person who's being asked about you. Most professionals don't intend for their network to give out fuzzy, garbled messages of who they are and what they can do, and how they are valued. Yet these vague answers happen every day.

Why? Because of lack of knowledge, lack of understanding, and lack of training in this area of networking. If you, like most people, still think networking is about whose name you can call up on your email or social networking account, you need to know that networking is about much more than that.

## 2. The Four Paramount Rules for Networking

**W**hen  most people think about networking, they envision attending dozens of  seminars in an effort to trade business cards with people they never intend to contact. After all, the more business cards you have in your Rolodex, the better off  you are, right?

Nothing could be further from the truth! Especially when you're networking with the aim of  supporting your personal brand. Understanding the value of  networking is only the first step in the process. It doesn't help much if  you don't know how to actually network successfully.

You can follow a number of  techniques to create and build your personal brand, and many of  these techniques have fancy names—for example, impression management, reputation management, and reputation capital. But every single one of  these hinges on your professional network. It doesn't matter what the face of your personal brand looks like if you have a pile of skeletons in the closet.

Having a strong network in place will ensure that your brand is genuine and also that there are no questions about it. Your network will be made up of people who can and will attest that the brand you put out there really is what it says it is. Just consider your network to be a list of a company's satisfied customers.

When it comes to networking, you've got several ways to go about it. Some people just seem to be natural connectors, while others have to work harder at it. Whichever one you are, it's important to follow these four paramount rules for networking.

**Rule #1: Don't just swap business cards.**

It's true that you will be in some situations where everyone is trading business cards, and that's fine. But you'll never actually add anyone to your network by simply exchanging cards.

Think about that stack of business cards you have already. Would you feel comfortable calling any of those people and asking them for a favor, such as whether it is okay to list you as a reference or request a professional introduction?

You probably don't even have a clue about the wide range of names in that stack of cards. In fact, I'll bet you can't even name half of the people whose cards are living in your

Rolodex or in a rubber-banded bundle in your desk drawer. A stack of business cards does not a network make.

Recently I spoke to a travel association about branding and networking. A member of the audience approached me afterward, gave me a business card, and enthusiastically talked about my presentation. We corresponded and eventually connected on LinkedIn. I requested a recommendation from her regarding my presentation. She wrote the recommendation, and now I have a testimonial that over 100 million people can read on LinkedIn. This is how I leveraged much more than swapping a business card.

**Rule #2: Choose the people you want to be in your network.**

If you are at an event where there's a lot of card swapping going on, make special note of the cards belonging to people you would like to connect with. These are the people you feel would make useful additions to your network. By making conscious decisions about whom you'd like to add to your network, you're creating valuable contacts within your industry.

For example, let's say you're at a three-day IT conference in Chicago where the top brains in the IT world are gathered. You spot someone wearing a nametag saying he is a VP for a prestigious IT company that you are interested in. You have considered working for this company in the past and now the opportunity to get a true feel for the company is standing in front of you at this conference. It's also an opportune time to put your best foot forward.

The people you hone in on should be those you have things in common with. It should be easy to converse with these individuals because there's a lot to talk about. Perhaps you are both coworkers within the same industry, or maybe you both enjoy the same hobbies. This type of information can be learned through quick online research via your smartphone or iPad as well as attentive listening and observation. If you get a glance at a nametag, you can quickly type in the name via your web browser and look for professional details and commonalities on the person's LinkedIn profile.

If you are at a conference, there is a good chance there is a website or a brochure with bios for the participants. This could be another valuable resource. Research the names online. You'll find plenty to talk about once you approach the person.

Another smart rule of thumb is to connect with people you know well enough that you would be completely comfortable writing a recommendation for. This helps to protect the integrity of your connections and strengthens your entire network. I have been contacted numerous times as a reference for members of my network, and it is an honor to provide a positive recommendation. This is part of paying it forward. It would be embarrassing and reflect poorly on me if I received a call for a connection from someone I didn't know.

**Rule #3: Let the chase begin.**

You'll have to put some effort into your network if you want to truly develop it. Once you've identified the people you could share things with, it's time to actually go after them and develop that relationship. They might not be good networkers, or they may not even be thinking about making connections. Whatever the case, it will usually be up to you to make the first contact.

Remember that IT exec you met at the conference in Chicago? Send him a letter referencing the time you met. Connect with him over LinkedIn and send a personal message with your invitation to join you on LinkedIn. Emailing works too, or a phone call may also be effective if the connection is strong.

Just explore and find the best way you connect with other people. Then use that method to set up lunches or other meetings with the people you want to strengthen your connection with. This is how you build relationships and create a strong network of people who not only know you, but will also back up your personal brand when asked about you.

**Rule #4: Look for opportunities to partner with each other.**

Part of true networking is being able to create opportunities together. By partnering with someone on a project, you give him or her an opportunity to work directly with you, and the level of what you can accomplish together will be much higher than what you could do alone!

Take a look at the nonprofit community for an example. The strongest nonprofit organizations have partnerships with businesses and other nonprofits. In fact, grant-making foundations are less likely to give funds to an organization attempting to operate on its own without any strategic partnerships. This is because partnerships make both halves of the relationship infinitely stronger and better. There is so much more you will be able to do because you build up that particular network connection and make it even stronger.

By creating together, you make it more likely that the other person will recommend you to others. You'll also add on some incredible projects to your résumé, further enhancing your personal brand.

## 3. Me, Inc.

In a day and age when taking control of your career is not only essential, but highly possible, you won't want to leave anything to chance. And the only way you will be driven to action with regard to the health of your network is to have a full understanding of its value.

Once you grasp how valuable your network is, you will set about to nurture and grow that network in an effective and efficient way using the four paramount rules of networking.

Networking is a continuous process. You should always be on the lookout for people you can help and be helped by. This mutual exchange should be happening all the time— before, during, and after your personal brand is in place.

But even before the network can serve you well, you must know who you are, what you want, and where you are going. You need to be the founding member of Me, Inc. If you've already been using your network to find strategic partners in projects that are important for you, then you already have an indication about what's important to you. Use that inkling to figure out the rest of the equation.

# SHIFT HAPPENS

You've heard that old saying, "If you don't know where you're going, how will you know when you get there?" Never is it more true than in planning the direction of your career path. So if you are using the same old paths that your parents and grandparents traveled, you are in for a rude awakening.

Perhaps you still think that your manager, or your CEO or even the board of directors, is in control of your future. Or perhaps you assume that company stock prices, satisfied (or dissatisfied) customers, or the company's profit and loss statements determine the security of your present position.

This is absolutely not true in today's workplace.

It's time for a total paradigm shift! Such thinking places you in a victim mode with victim mentality, both of which can be lethal. While you may be thinking that things are getting worse and worse, there are others around you who are delirious with excitement and anticipation due to what is available in self-promotion and personal branding tools.

This concept is very difficult for Baby Boomers, especially the female half of that generation. Traditionally, the belief was that you got a job and stuck with it until the day they gave you the gold watch and retirement cake, but that simply isn't the case anymore. About a third of workers in the United States will change jobs every twelve months. By the time you reach the age of forty-two (if you haven't already), you probably will have had about ten jobs, according to the Department of Labor.

If you're forty-two or older and reading this, think back to your very first job and consider how many jobs you've had. Then think about how many involved a complete career change.

Each time you took a different job, you reinvented yourself, whether you knew it or not. Changing where you work is about more than simply reporting to a new workplace each day. Sometimes reinventing involves a move across the country or leveraging new skills. But to be eligible for these advancements, you have to not only know who you are, but also know how to tell others who you are and learn how to market yourself to the employers you want to work for.

Every year that you age, the more entrenched you may feel in your current job. You may feel that you have complete job security, but sometimes there's a surprise right around the corner. Are you prepared?

# ANT OR GRASSHOPPER?

There are those who have seen a shift coming and, like the ant in the fable of the grasshopper and the ant, have been diligently storing away vital information, building key relationships, and showcasing their talents and abilities with websites, blogs, and social media. Meanwhile the grasshopper is flitting about simply thankful to have a job to go to each day. The most work the grasshopper does is to maintain the status quo.

Every year or so that grasshopper gets out the old résumé and dusts it off and makes a few updates, but in the event of a day of reckoning, he is ill-prepared. He never thinks about the next rung on his success ladder until it's too late. One pink slip and it's all over.

When that moment comes, it's "fall back" time. That means the ill-prepared grasshopper *falls back* on all the old methods: calling up and connecting with recruiters, updating and posting the résumé, creating new cover letters, struggling to remember past contacts, searching all the online job boards and so on. You get the picture.

While just a few people keep their résumés and networks updated in case the unexpected happens, even fewer are making conscious efforts to brand themselves and seek out new opportunities.

Among the Baby Boomer generation, we scarcely see workers jumping out and making themselves known as they seek that next big position. This may be because they have gotten comfortable with their jobs. Getting comfortable is dangerous because it leads to slacking off. It doesn't take long before that résumé is collecting dust in the digital file drawer.

Like grasshoppers, we begin to define ourselves as our current position at the company we currently work for, but there is so much more out there for those who focus on branding themselves.

Companies spend millions of dollars developing a brand, and that brand brings in billions of dollars over its life. Of course you don't need to spend that kind of money to develop your brand. Instead, what you are going to be spending is time. Developing a solid brand takes both time and money, but with individuals, the time cost is much higher than the monetary cost.

## SNOOZERS LOSE

Believe it: In this work climate, if you snooze, you *will* lose. While you are fumbling and stumbling around, others are nearing the finish line. (Possibly with something as innovative as a video résumé ready for instant presentation!)

There is a better way for you. It's time to take control of your own career by identifying and developing your unique persona or *brand*.

Are you ready and willing to be promoted to the CEO of Me, Inc.? If so, the first step is to find out how much you actually know about your company. What exactly is Me, Inc., all about? If you have not done so recently, you will need to set aside a period of quiet time in order to make your assessments. One session is imperative; several sessions will work even better.

## WHO ARE YOU?

Create a Me, Inc., notebook in which you can make needed notes. You will want to begin by reviewing all of your strengths. Make a list of the following strengths and include your abilities too:

- **What are you good at?** Do you like to analyze data? Are you an event organizer? Do you coach and mentor others?
- **Why do you stand out in the crowd?** Do you have a positive demeanor? Is your appearance professional?
- **What differentiates you and makes you memorable?** Do you ask thoughtful questions? Are you a good listener? Are you punctual?
- **What do people most appreciate about you?** What type of feedback do you hear? What are you asked most

frequently to do? What type of role are you typically attracted to?

- **What do others say regarding your abilities and personality?** Have you had assessments done? What have these revealed? How do you express your personality? Is it written word or verbal?

- **When you're involved in a team project, what do you bring to the table that is totally unique to you?** Is it your sense of humor? Your compassion for others? Your extraordinary ability to see the big picture? Your penchant for details? Your creativity?

Roll these questions around in your mind until you can create your list. This list of strengths and abilities will point to your unique value(s). Your unique value will form the foundation for Me, Inc.

If, while creating this list, your areas of weakness keep coming to mind, you may have to spend a little longer in formulating your list of strengths. They are there—perhaps neglected and ignored, but they are there.

Branding is, putting it succinctly, knowing who you are.

## What Is Your Personal Brand Statement?

Once this list is completed, it's time to move to the next step of stating your vision. Some people call this a mission statement. Since the subject of branding has become more and more common, some are calling this your "Personal Brand Statement." What you call it is immaterial. That

## Something to Wrap Your Noodle Around

Here are some examples of personal brand statements:

- I'm a problem solver, consultant, and author on workplace issues, human capital management, and work/life balance.
- Finance expert with 20+ years in Private Equity and Investment Banking.
- Creative freelance artist with over two decades of experience in painting, drawing, and pottery.

Now it's your turn to create your personal brand statement:

_____

you create one is what's important. Your personal brand statement should consist of only one sentence—two at the most—and should incorporate your unique values that you have identified.

While this statement can be somewhat fluid, it will be the cornerstone on which you will build your brand profile.

You may want to write several and then ask a few trusted friends and colleagues to give you feedback. Which one would they select that fits you best?

Once your personal brand statement is complete, you can use this in your résumé; in your biography (bio); as part of your signature on emails; on sites such as Facebook, LinkedIn, and ZoomInfo; and to title your blog and your personal website. In other words, this statement will form the common thread that runs through all of your brand-creating tools that will be at your disposal. This statement will set you apart and make you distinguishable from others so that you stand out from the crowd.

Your personal brand statement should be easy to remember and stand out. Employers will see it on your résumé, and they should be able to remember it easily without trying to do so. Later, when they begin scheduling interviews, they may not remember your name at first because you're one of hundreds of candidates applying for the job, but they will remember your brand statement because it makes a much more memorable impression than just a name.

## What Do You Want?

To recognize what it is you want in life means identifying your deep-felt passion. If you think you have to sacrifice passion in order to have a career, think again. One of the key elements of creating your own brand is to find your passion and let it shine.

People who live their passions are people who are alive, vibrant, and full of energy. Those are the kinds of people who are noticed; those are the kinds of people that many employers are looking for.

What would you like to accomplish by using the unique gifts with which you have been endowed? Perhaps that cannot be accomplished here and now in the position you currently hold, but if you begin to cultivate that vision, you will begin to move toward it. As you cultivate your vision, ideas and opportunities will begin to appear to you.

## Where Are You Going?

If you are now employed, do you have visions of moving up in the company? Or have you set your sights on another place, another position, and would like to move out of your situation altogether? Or is it your goal to simply lift yourself out of the mundane and become memorable to those around you—not only in the workplace, but in your local community and in the global community as well? Perhaps you are the entrepreneur who is looking to break free and start your own business.

As stated in the opening of this chapter, if you don't know where you're going, how will you know when you get there? It's sad but true that individuals who have no direction usually find themselves wasting time doing mundane tasks that have no long-range benefit in their lives. When you have focus, purpose, and clear direction, it's like having a roadmap in hand for every day of your life. Each day you know what must be accomplished to move you nearer to those goals you have set.

# GOAL SETTING

Goal setting may be one of the scariest parts of personal branding, simply because it involves thinking about change. If you have become comfortable in your current position, it's time to begin making yourself feel uncomfortable. Shoot for the stars and decide what you want to achieve. If you've already achieved your goals, then you're aiming too low.

The subject of goal setting is much too broad to be sufficiently covered within the scope of this book, but the power of setting goals cannot be overlooked or minimized. Once you have identified your values and your passions, your goal-setting exercise should become much easier. And all of these should be closely intertwined.

Any goal setting should include goals that are both short-range and long-range. They can cover your personal life as well as your career. Some people go so far as to create actual *life* goals, and then structure their life game plan in sets of five-year segments: *Where would I like to be, what would I like to be doing in five years, ten years, fifteen years and so on.*

When creating your goals list, use the SMART acronym.

Make sure your goals are

**S**pecific—Know exactly what you want to accomplish.

**M**easurable—How will you quantify your progress?

**A**ttainable—Your goal should be a challenge but make sure it is achievable.

**R**ealistic—Are you willing to fully focus and commit to the goal?

**T**imely—The timeline should have a clearly defined start and end date with checkpoints if applicable.

A basic goal may be: I want to lose weight. But a SMART goal for the same topic would be: I want to lose ten pounds by New Year's Eve. I will do a cardio workout three to four times a week for thirty minutes, and I will cut out all sweets from my diet.

If your goal is too vague, or has no deadlines, or is totally unrealistic, the chances of attaining that goal are slim.

As you grow in the process of networking to build your personal brand, the more you know about Me, Inc., the more effective you will be in communicating that with others around you. Soon your persona will be going forth with less and less of your effort, both by word of mouth and online. It begins to take on a momentum of its own, which is discussed in chapter 4.

Another effective technique is called vision mapping. Essentially if you can focus your view on what you would like to achieve, your goal becomes more of a motivator toward your success. Vision maps are created by finding pictures that represent what you are trying to achieve. They are glued together on a large piece of poster board to create your map. Much like a collage of magazine clippings and pictures printed from the Internet, these maps are usually placed in a position (your cubicle wall or bathroom mirror or refrigerator) where you can view it frequently as a reminder of your goal.

For the goal of weight loss, just described, the vision map could include pictures that include a party dress you want to wear, a Zumba class, and a target weight number. With a deadline of New Year's Eve, the vision map could also include pictures surrounding New Year's festivities.

For a goal of, say, a new job in advertising, your vision map might include company logos you'd like to work on, a diploma for that MBA you're working on, and a corner office setting.

# 4. From Web 1.0 to Web 2.0 and Beyond

**W**hile the world of technology was trembling in fearful anticipation of a Y2K crash at the dawn of the new millennium, what actually happened was what came to be known as the "dot com bust." In January 2000, the first "domino" fell, creating a chain reaction that resulted in the loss of $5 trillion in market value of technology companies in less than two years.

The Internet honeymoon was definitely over, and many proclaimed the demise of the World Wide Web. However, rather than going into total oblivion, the stage and the scenes of the Internet were altered and changed.

## GEN X TO GEN Y

A discussion regarding the changes in technology cannot truly be thorough without at least a passing reference to these two strong post–Baby Boom generations. They have come to be known as Generation X and Generation Y. While both of these groups have grown up with PCs, the Internet, and technology in general, there remain broad differences in their views.

The Gen Xers are the first generation following the Baby Boomers. They were born between the mid-sixties to the late seventies. While many of these individuals are computer savvy (many were building their own computers in high school), most have had to double-step to keep up with recent advances in technology. Now in their late thirties to mid-forties, they may have enough disposable income to contract out much of their technology-related services such as podcasting, blogging, and creating websites.

Gen Y, on the other hand, live and breathe their iPods and Blackberries and have been tech savvy from kindergarten up. These folks were born on the heels of the Gen Xers and are sometimes referred to as Generation Next or Echo Boomers because they are often children of Baby Boomers.

| Years: | Generation Title: |
|---|---|
| 1925-1942 | Silent Generation |
| 1943-1964 | Baby Boomer Generation |
| 1965-1976 | Generation X |
| 1977-1994 | Generation Y |

The issue that seems to be unfolding for Gen Xers and also Baby Boomers (an overlap in categories) is that they are growing lax and getting too comfortable in the positions they hold, which leaves them vulnerable when catastrophe strikes. Whether that comes in the form of company downsizing, sellouts, company closings, or whatever else, few are using this present moment to get prepared. They've had the same job for decades and don't see it going anywhere. They believe, just as their parents did, that once you get a job with a company, you stay with that company for the duration of your career. (The grasshopper mentality, remember?)

But in today's world, this just isn't the case any longer. As a whole, our society is more mobile than ever before. We're actively moving, switching homes, trading jobs. We're all over the map. Consequently, you're not just vying for jobs with other people in your own neighborhood. You're up against anyone else in the world who wants the same job you want. This makes the world not only feel smaller, but larger at the same time. Personal branding is what makes you stand out against the world. While some Baby Boomers and

Gen Xers are aware of personal branding, few are jumping in to make it happen.

It is the Gen Y individuals who are much more flexible and can see clearly that they must look out for themselves. As you read further about the transformation from Web 1.0 to Web 2.0, you'll easily identify where each group fits, and you'll identify yourself in the process.

## THE TRANSFORMATION

In the nineties, the Internet was a spectator sport. Those who surfed the Web visited a website, which was static. Blogs were essentially online diaries that were not exactly user-friendly. Few people had the skills to create one, let alone maintain one. Companies used the Internet as a place to tout their wares, but there was little or no feedback. No interaction; no conversation.

If an individual wanted his or her own website, it meant paying big bucks to a web designer. There were no simple do-it-yourself Web design programs available.

Everything that had to do with the Internet was largely static and one dimensional.

Compare this also to the work landscape where workers were ensconced in cubicle farms within their corporate structure and taught to meld into the woodwork as it were. Conforming was the rule, and personal branding (if one had even heard of it) was definitely an exception. Individuality was not encouraged.

## Web 2.0

Contrary to the doomsayers' proclamations, the Internet did not die following the bust. Instead it evolved and continued to grow by leaps and bounds. Every day more and more people are surfing the Web to shop, to meet friends, to communicate, to get information—the list is endless. Hundreds of millions of people in the U.S. alone surf the Web on a daily basis.

The biggest difference when comparing today against the nineties is the community-driven environment that has emerged. No longer is the Internet static or one dimensional; it is definitely a two-way street. It was through this evolution that the term *social media* came into being.

When you think of Web 2.0, think of two-way communication. When the Internet first evolved, it was geared to push data to people. It was a one-way dialogue. Websites pushed data to the audience and interaction with the audience did not exist. Web 2.0, on the other hand, is very interactive. It is a multi-channel conversation. You can talk to one person or to thousands depending on the Internet tool you are using.

## Social Media

Although a very general term, social media is thought of as areas such as Internet forums, blogs, social blogs, wikis, podcasts, pictures, video, and bookmarking. These involve technologies such as blogs, picture-sharing, vlogs, wall-postings, email, instant messaging, music-sharing, and voice over IP.

Today even the most technology-challenged person can set up a website and start a personal blog. Beyond that, millions of everyday people take active part in social interchange sites such as Facebook.

It was inevitable, then, that these changes would eventually bleed over into the corporate landscape and the work world. If you are serious about building your career and protecting your future, you cannot afford to be ignorant about social media.

As more and more recruiting professionals begin using such sites as LinkedIn to search for and find employees, how can you afford not to be highly visible in these arenas?

Without a doubt, Web 2.0 and social media are obliterating the old methods of career management and development. This can either appear as a threat to you or as a wide open, limitless opportunity.

Essentially, this means that you are now in command of your career and can steer it in the direction that you

## Food for Thought

A **blog** (think of combining **web** and **log** to form **blog**) is a website or area on a website that contains your original content or observations that you update periodically. You can include video and other graphics such as photos. Bloggers try to write interesting information that attracts a following, and visitors can often leave comments about what is written in a blog entry. Some blogs are commentaries on political or business topics. Others may be more personal such as a daily update on someone's cancer treatment. You can use your blog to promote your brand by sharing your expertise on a subject. So **vlogs**, then, are video versions of blogs, and YouTube is commonly used for these vlogs. There are more than 150 million blogs on the web—and growing.

A **wiki** is a tool that enables open communication, updated in "real time," among many people with open access. Users can modify the content. Wikipedia is an example of a huge wiki.

**Podcasting** refers to the technology used to pull digital audio files from websites down to computers and devices such as MP3 players. Podcast is derived from the name of the iPod MP3 player from Apple, although you don't need an iPod to listen to podcasts.

A **vodcast** is the video version of a podcast. These can be downloaded to a computer or iPod. YouTube videos may be considered vodcasts.

**Bookmarking** in the technology world is much like dog-earing a page in a book. Users store their favorite sites or Internet shortcuts so they can go there quickly and easily. You may have shortcuts stored in your Favorites folder. Now these bookmarks can be shared with others, through social bookmarking. If you and others have similar interests, you can store your bookmarks on a web-based bookmarking service to let other users access them.

**Voice over Internet Protocol** (Voice over IP, also expressed as VoIP) refers to technology that allows communication such as phone calls over the Internet.

determine by using networking to develop and enhance your personal brand. No longer must you hide in the shadow of your employer. No longer must you fade into the role of a mindless robot. You can utilize technology and social media to define who you are, create your personal brand, and begin to purposefully network to bring it all together.

You will either be **reactive** or **proactive**. You can either **let it happen**, or **make it happen**. It's up to you!

What are you going to do with this newfound power? Today you have power you never experienced before. No longer are you branded by the name or reputation of the company you work for. Now you have the power to create your own brand and be uniquely yourself—the perfect and only match for that job you want.

## 5. The Power of One

In the past, there was power in numbers, especially when you were talking about networks. The more influential people you knew, the better off you were. While this is still true today, there is far more power than just what is found in your network, even if it includes some very substantial connections with some influential people.

Today there is also power in you. You can connect to almost anyone you want to connect with in the world. It just may take a little bit of work on your part. You won't be able to make these connections tomorrow, but you can still make them if you just take some time to think about how you can get to the person you want to meet.

For example, let's say that you wanted to get in touch with your town's mayor. Initially you may attempt a phone call, but the likelihood of actually getting through to Mayor Smith is slim. If you wanted to get an email or perhaps get a message to him or her, you could look to your network. The mayor may even have a LinkedIn profile, which would make contact more likely. It probably wouldn't take that many steps to get in touch with the mayor, but you could easily do it just by looking at your own network and then figuring out the easiest route to get to him or her. The power of your network is right in the palm of your hand—if you know how to use it.

## SIX DEGREES

You may be familiar with the concept of "six degrees of separation." The term refers to the idea that if you are only one "step" away from each person you know and you are two steps away from each person known by one of the people *they* know, then you (and everyone else) are only six steps away from any other person on Earth.

Is this true? Can it be proven?

Various experiments throughout the years have indicated that there is a good chance that it can work, and today the number of steps it takes to get to someone else may be fewer than it was years ago. Some experts are predicting that it can take as few as two steps to make a connection that would have taken six steps to connect decades ago.

The fact is, we live in an incredibly shrinking world, and it's becoming smaller and more connected with each new click of the mouse. This is why it is so important that the image you portray—whether in person, at work, in a social setting or on the Web—is the image that you feel best expresses your finest qualities and the talents you have to offer.

The six degrees concept was first popularized by Karinthy Frigyes, a Hungarian author and playwright. In his 1929 short story entitled "Chains" he writes:

A fascinating game grew out of this discussion. One of us suggested performing the following experiment to prove that the population of the Earth is closer together now than they have ever been before. We should select any person from the 1.5 billion inhabitants of the Earth—anyone, anywhere at all. He bet us that, using no more than five individuals, one of whom is a personal acquaintance, he could contact the selected individual using nothing except the network of personal acquaintances.

That was 1929—almost a century ago. More recently, a game called the *Six Degrees of Kevin Bacon* has kept the idea in the forefront. The game was the result of a statement that actor Kevin Bacon made saying he'd "worked with everybody in Hollywood or someone who's worked with them." Three college students took the idea and ran with it. The object of the game is for a group of players to attempt to connect any screen actor in history to Kevin Bacon, and to do it as quickly and in as few links as possible.

Since the emergence of the game, Bacon has created a charitable organization named SixDegrees.org. This too plays on this idea of the "small world phenomenon" and to create a charitable social network that inspires other celebrities to give to charities online.

At first glance this information may only warrant from you a nonchalant shrug. But if you ponder it for any time at all, you will begin to see how really powerful it is. The idea that you are only six steps from anyone that you need to connect with on this planet can be empowering. And then if you are trained in how to capitalize on this idea and walk it out, nothing and no one is out of your reach.

## THE EMERGENCE OF SOCIAL MEDIA

Are you old enough to remember BBS (Bulletin Board System) on the Internet? How about such sites as CompuServe and the early days of AOL? These were some of the earliest steps of the working of a social media system on the Internet.

In the infant days of the Internet, the ether was inhabited by nerds who loved sitting for hours—all alone—in front of a computer. We called them "anti-social." But then such things as bulletin boards emerged through which people could actually communicate with one another. And most of them talked about computers and technology. (If you can imagine the phone line/modem/dial-up slowness of their interchanges, those were definitely the old days.)

CompuServe came along in the 1970s and offered the ability to exchange files and to access news and events. Although email was not new at the time, CompuServe made it much easier to send and receive. But then, CompuServe went a step further allowing their members to join discussion forums. These were an instant hit as people could discuss a wide range of subjects with hundreds and thousands of other people.

AOL was the pioneer in setting up member-created communities in addition to members' profiles that were actually searchable. Another step in the birth of what we know today as social media.

## An Ever-Growing Phenomenon

When you look at this history, it's certainly no surprise that what should follow are the more sophisticated sites we have today such as Facebook and LinkedIn. Facebook reigns supreme as the most popular, with users numbering above 150 million and counting.

The common denominator with such sites is the open communication channel that fosters a growing circle of friends, acquaintances, and contacts. Your sphere of influence is highly visible and brings a fresh, new awareness of just how small this world can really be.

Taking this power a step further, you should also have a fresh new awareness of the power that lies at your fingertips. With a few keystrokes and a few clicks of a mouse, you can begin to create your own personal brand and in effect raise your own level of credibility and marketability. You have the power to use your own sphere of influence to shape your personal and professional futures.

# 6. Social Media and Your Personal Brand

Today you can learn almost anything you want to learn just by doing a little research on the Internet, so why would you think this would be any different when it comes to others learning information about you?

You may not be anyone famous, but there is more information about you just floating around in cyberspace than what you're aware of. The good news is that you can control that information to a degree.

It's important to remember that changes in the workplace are occurring with such lightning speed that it requires a concerted effort to keep up. The fact is, in the near future, you won't go looking for a job because those employers will *find you.* (That is, *if you can be found!*) Having an online presence is essential for your personal brand.

## YOUR NAME DOMAIN

You already know about the importance of creating the company called Me, Inc. You need to know who you are, what you want, and where you are going. Add to that the knowledge of what you stand for. All of these attributes can be reflected in your online presence.

One of the first things you will want to do to establish your identity online is to own your domain: "yourname.com." If you have a common name, think of ways to differentiate yourself such as the use of an initial.

Another option might be using the idea you want to express about yourself and creating a domain that way. For example, if you've got two strong power words within your brand message, you might consider building a website around that and incorporating your name into it. This will help you stand out even more from other people who have the same name as you.

Once you own your own domain, use it, or an extension of it, in all that you do online for such uses as your personal website, blog site, in articles, press releases, in your email signature and so on. You may want to create an email account at gmail (Google's own) and set it up as: firstname. lastname@gmail.com.

For example, my website is AuthorAprilKelly.com. Again, you want to create an image of consistency and reliability.

Also if you have not done so, you will need your own logo to use on your site. For this you may need to hire a graphic artist. Be patient and take the time to create a logo you can live with. You'll use it to represent your image in many different arenas both online and offline.

## You Will Be Googled—Like It or Not

Another aspect of your online Web presence isn't about what you put out there yourself. It's about what other sources put out about you. Human resource professionals are being trained to conduct online searches for information on candidates for jobs. And the first place most will go is to Google; then they go to sites such as LinkedIn and ZoomInfo for more detailed professional information. What do you look like on a Google search? (That dilemma will be discussed in greater detail in a later chapter.)

Statistics show that when people are looking for the name of a business associate or colleague, most will go straight to Google. It is by far the most-used search engine on the Internet. How well has your "goodwill ambassador" (that is, your network) represented you? And how well is your network "commodity" growing in value?

The only way to find out what's out there about you on the Internet is to do your own research. Have you Googled yourself lately? If not, why not? In order to build your own strong personal brand, you need to know what is already floating around in cyberspace that bears your name. Believe it or not, even this information is somewhat controllable, even though you don't have direct control over it. More on that later.

If you don't like what you see (or don't see), Google has introduced a feature called "Google profile." This is quite similar to Facebook where you can create your own profile that will then appear at the bottom of all U.S. name-query search pages.

This is great news for professionals who want to build their personal brand online. You will want to create your Google profile at plus.google.com by including your name, occupation, and location (and professional photo as well). This short bio will appear on the first page of the search results for your name. From there the visitor is led to a link to your full Google profile page. And in Google-type wisdom, the Google profile page is designed so that the more info you add to your profile, the higher up in the page ranking you will appear. (More about your actual Google ranking in a later chapter.)

It's quick, easy, and free. No reason not to use this new feature. And then be sure to Google yourself often to keep abreast of what is being said (or printed) about you.

You'll also notice when you Google yourself that you'll come up with a list of other professionals who happen to have the same name as you. For example, if you Google me, you'll discover that there is also a television producer and writer by the same name. I'm certainly not the April Kelly who co-created the *Boy Meets World* television series, so I've got to be able to distinguish myself from her.

One of the ways I have done this is through my LinkedIn profile. When you conduct a search, you'll see that my LinkedIn profile will pop up and you will notice my location—Omaha, NE—and the subtitle to my profile, which describes me: Senior Consultant, Author, Speaker.

Personal branding is what allows you to set yourself apart from all the other people with the same name. If you are one of the lucky few without a common name, then your task is a bit easier, but it becomes enormously more difficult for people with a last name like Smith or Jones. Wherever you fall on the name continuum, personal branding will protect you from others being mistaken as you. The whole idea behind branding is "accept no substitutes."

Including a professional photo of yourself on all your online profiles is essential because it can help to cut down on this issue, but it's not bulletproof. What about the people who have no idea what you look like? This is where a catchy brand message and a profile that accurately reflects your strengths and passions comes in, and LinkedIn is the perfect place to create this professional profile.

LinkedIn profiles do come up in Google searches of your name. In fact, you'll discover an entire list of professionals with your name on your Google search. The professionals who have clearly spelled out who they are and what they do are more likely to be "found."

## WHY LINKEDIN IS DIFFERENT

As you are building your online personal brand, you definitely will be including a number of social media tools. These might include Facebook, Twitter, MySpace, and Yahoo! Groups. Into this group, for a more professional social networking site, you will want to include LinkedIn. Often you read about LinkedIn lumped with other social media sites. But it is not the same. LinkedIn has a much different purpose and design than any others.

Why and how is LinkedIn different? First, it is specifically designed for business professionals and business owners rather than for the general public. By creating your profile on LinkedIn, you can summarize all of your professional accomplishments and showcase your qualifications, talents, goals, interests, and abilities (very much like a résumé on steroids). Because it's searchable in many ways, you will want to add your areas of expertise and use keywords and phrases that allow your skills to be found.

Earlier I mentioned how exponential growth can occur in online networking. That snowball effect can definitely happen for you by utilizing all the features of LinkedIn. That is, if you know and understand how to correctly tap into the features of this amazing site.

Let's clear up some of the confusion surrounding LinkedIn—specifically about what it is and what it can do. Some professionals come into the site with the belief that it's the magic wand that will give them access to all the shakers and movers out there in their particular field or industry. Others mistakenly try to use it in ways that are familiar to them—like they would Facebook. Still others think that if they are set up on LinkedIn they can slack off on other modes and methods of networking (definitely not so).

In the next major section of this book, I take you inside LinkedIn, showing you step by step how to make it work for you.

# Part Two
## The Main Course

## 7. Begin with Your LinkedIn Profile

**M**ost professionals never realize the doors that can open up if they just learn how to network professionally on LinkedIn. With all the social networking sites out there, LinkedIn is where you can get the most bang for your buck when it comes to your professional life.

LinkedIn is by far the most important social networking site for professionals because it involves much more than just tossing up a profile and connecting with friends or coworkers. LinkedIn is a more professional environment than other social networking sites, and it provides many more opportunities for you professionally.

What scares most people about LinkedIn, however, is that they don't know how to use it. The site is so different from other social networking sites that most people seem to be confused about the best way to tap into its power.

Most users throw up an incomplete profile and end up just scratching the surface of what they can do on the site.

Of course, the foundation of using LinkedIn starts with your profile, and that's where you'll start before you really get into the nitty gritty of the site.

## LAY THE FOUNDATION FIRST

Entering into the LinkedIn site can be both exciting and terrifying. Add to that the fact that it can be somewhat overwhelming. This is why I never suggest that anyone set up a LinkedIn account until all the foundational work (as outlined in the previous chapters) has been completed. Only when you know who you are, know what you want, and know where you are going can you effectively use the services of LinkedIn.

Those who jump in and throw together a hodgepodge of information, incorporating long, boring lists of accomplishments, and use their site to collect contacts like baseball cards are headed for great disappointment. They are the ones who will be quick to say that LinkedIn "isn't all it's cracked up to be."

Why do certain individuals choose to be a part of the LinkedIn landscape in the first place? There are many reasons. Some want to enhance their professional online presence (in other words, their personal branding). Others want to expand their network of valuable contacts.

Recruiters use it to find candidates for positions, and the jobless are looking for those positions. Still others enjoy the immense opportunities for learning that LinkedIn provides. (A vast storehouse of knowledge is available in the LinkedIn Answers area, which offers answers to questions from a wide variety of categories such as communications and business travel.)

Basically, LinkedIn can be what you need it to be, but the key is you must know what you need!

If you've invested the time required to lay the right foundation, then you're ready to go into the site and set up your profile.

## CREATING YOUR PROFILE

While LinkedIn is not the only business networking site online, it is by far the most popular and the most populated. When you log on, you will find that there are free memberships and "premium" plans. The main advantage of the latter is more powerful search tools and enhanced access. Only you can gauge which will be best for you.

After signing in to your account, you'll be at the member home page and this is where you will begin to build your profile. Think of the immense advantage of writing your own profile where you have full editorial rights and you control the content. It's yours—all yours. This is the place where you can let your personal voice come forth and let your personal brand show. No need for dry corporate-speak here.

Recall the projects and activities in which you have been involved and those that might not have seen the light of day without your presence. Review what makes you excited and revs up your enthusiasm. Here's where you can showcase what your colleagues and superiors have to say about you. Your values and your authenticity come to the surface. Don't try to complete this in one sitting, but rather let it be a fluid, growing process. Play with it and have fun. Remember, it's all yours. It's Me, Inc!

## Information for Your Profile

What types of information will you need to gather in order to complete a thorough and informative profile?

- Your résumé including your work history, your present position, and title
- Extracurricular activities you've been involved in
- Groups and organizations of which you are an active member
- Volunteer work you have done
- Your education history

- A profile summary (here you will include a professional, business-type photo)
- Specialties—gifts and talents that make you memorable and set you apart from others
- Recommendations from other members of LinkedIn (more about how to obtain these later on in the book)

Think in terms of balance: You don't want to have so much information that reading it becomes laborious. On the other hand, you will want to have enough information so that friends, recruiters, hiring managers, or potential business partners can find you.

## YOUR FACE

It's important to have a photo of yourself so that people can see who you are. This is not the time for a quick snapshot snatched from the family album. Invest in a professional photographer and discuss with him or her exactly what you want the photo to communicate about you and your personal brand. Ask other professionals for referrals in this area. Make sure there will be a wide range of images for you to choose from. Ask the opinion of trusted colleagues which shots they feel best express who you are.

Your photo helps people put a face with the name and makes you come alive on the Web. By using a professional photo as part of your brand-identity system, you will thereby develop a deeper connection with your audience. Once you have a professional photo in hand, it can be used in all of your media tools, which also gives an aura of consistency and permanence.

## HOW TO BE FOUND

The more you add to your profile, the higher the chances of your information being accessed by other key people, which equates into more opportunities that will come your way.

If in the past you've created a well-crafted résumé, then you will have no trouble putting together a lively and appealing profile that others will want to read. The main difference here is that your LinkedIn profile will be indexed by the big search engines such as Google and Yahoo! You can optimize the indexing process by using full names of schools, colleges, universities, companies where you have worked, and your technical skills. Avoid using acronyms and initials.

Once your profile is completed you can then make the decision whether your profile will be visible to certain LinkedIn members or to anyone who browses the Internet.

And now you are ready to begin the networking process.

# 8. Building Your Network

The LinkedIn environment changes the general rules of networking a bit by adding another tier to the process. You may choose to keep someone in your LinkedIn network just to stay in touch with that person because you never know when a contact will come in handy.

However, you also can't expect to just contact those in your LinkedIn network whenever you need something. It is still up to you to forge those strategic business relationships and strengthen them in person instead of just over LinkedIn.

But let's start at the beginning with LinkedIn, creating your network from scratch.

## WHO DO YOU KNOW?

The main goal and purpose of working through your LinkedIn site is to build a quality network of contacts. How you go about this building process is strictly up to you. Everyone's goals are different. Some approach the networking process by importing all their contacts from all their email accounts, such as Outlook, Hotmail, Gmail, and others, and inviting them to join LinkedIn.

A word of warning here. If you receive too many "I don't know" clicks (meaning the recipient does not recognize your name), you could lose invitation privileges. So move slowly. The best route to take, if you are going to make blanket invitations, is to prepare your contacts ahead of time by informing them of what you are planning to do and why.

Keep in mind that as your site and your contacts grow, you too will begin to receive invitations. Decide ahead of time how you will sort through these and how you will accept or decline. Again, it all goes back to what your goals are and what will best serve the building of your personal brand online.

As you begin, think of people you work with, or have volunteered with, or perhaps were together in your college fraternity or sorority or other organizations in which you were an active member. Begin making those searches and contacts and move out from there.

# PUT YOUR BEST SELF FORWARD

LinkedIn provides a "canned" default invitation, but why use something so impersonal when there is a check box that says, "Add a personal note to your invitation"? This is part of your "first impression" plan in which you are putting your best *self* forward in the best light possible. And that includes making your invitations distinctive and personal.

Perhaps you want to connect with key personnel in an industry in which you are interested. While you may not know that person or have a history with him or her, it's simple to add your explanation in your invitation and let the recipient decide if he or she wants to reciprocate.

As an example, a job seeker used this wording in an invitation she sent out:

---

## Invitation

Dear Cindy,

Hello, my name is Sally Smith, and I noticed we are both involved in the same Marketing group here on LinkedIn. I am currently looking for a new opportunity with a progressive company. I have always admired the customer-first attitude of XYZ company, and I would like to connect with you in hopes of learning more about XYZ.

I appreciate your time and consideration. I hope you will respond positively to my invitation to connect.

Sincerely, Sally Smith (555) 555-5555

## MANAGING YOUR LIST

As your list of contacts grows, you may feel the need to manage the list. That means making a few removals. This is possible and easy. And while it does remove that connection for the time being, you can re-invite the contact at any time in the future. Most people don't notice they've been removed.

The invitations, on the other hand, can simply be archived. As this list grows, you won't want all these invitations cluttering up the page. For instance, go through the list and select those from whom you have not received a response and archive them to get them out of your way. You can do the same with received and blocked invitations.

## DEGREES OF SEPARATION

As you move and work within the world of LinkedIn, you will run into many references to "degrees of separation." This structure is extremely important, and it's not difficult to understand. I referred earlier to the concept of six degrees of separation. LinkedIn has done a takeoff on that concept.

Quite simply, those who are in your network are your first-degree connections. This creates the width of your networking. Of course each one of these connections has his or her own first-degree connections. That level then is your second-degree group. Next comes all of the connections of those connections, which creates those who

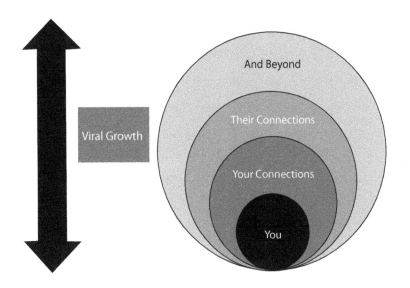

are three degrees away from you. As you can see, this process is capable of creating incredible growth in numbers.

On your LinkedIn site, you can view all of these connections to the third degree. However, you can only contact those in your third-degree level by requesting through the person between you and the third-level individual. Perhaps that person will pass on the request, perhaps not. You may have to do a little more research if you are adamant that this is a person with whom you want to build an online relationship.

It is advised (and sometimes required) that you have a good, solid relationship with those between you and that person you want to meet. In real life, you wouldn't recommend someone whose work you don't know, and the same holds true on LinkedIn. Don't expect someone to bend over backwards to connect you with someone you want to meet if you haven't taken the time to bring your connection person into your network completely. Spend some time getting to know that person first and look for ways to help him or her. This way you're contacting them with an offer of assistance rather than a request for help.

The advantages of viewing and reviewing those who are in your network are limitless. Perhaps a person in your network is employed at a company in which you have a great interest, and you see that in her network is one of the key personnel in that company. What better way to begin to lay the groundwork for a relationship?

Because of the amazing search options offered through LinkedIn, you can use "Degrees and Recommendations" as one of the parameters for a search. (More about recommendations in the next chapter.) This means you can search in the level you prefer.

## 1 + 1 = 4

Degrees of separation can help you gauge how your networking is growing and if you need to spend more quality time building it.

When you are on LinkedIn, for example, the navigation bar is on the top and one of the areas will say **Contacts**. If you click on this tab, your secondary menu has four options and the last one is titled **Network Statistics**. Clicking on this tab will tell you how large your network is. It includes your connections, your second-degree and your third-degree. It will also show you how many people have been added to your entire network in the last day.

In my case, I have 968 first-degree connections, 389,100 second-degree connections, and 11,703,400 third-degree connections. My total network is currently over 12 million strong and over 35,000 people were added in the last day. These are big numbers and show the power of viral growth.

If you stop for a moment and consider the power of this system, LinkedIn is staggering. While there is a great deal of power in your circle of friends, acquaintances, coworkers, old classmates, and so on, think of how that power increases when you are now connected to every person with whom *they* are connected. It becomes *unconventional math*: 1+1=4 and *more*. Quite literally, not only are the total number of contacts innumerable, but so are the advantages of using this system.

Connections are helpful, but how about getting those connections to recommend you? You can tap into the power of LinkedIn for recommendations, which is the subject of the next chapter.

# 9. Using Recommendations

**D**on't you just love a well-written, sincere referral letter?

In years past, we used to collect letters of referral, neatly copy them, and place them carefully in our portfolios. You never knew when you might need them for job hunting or when seeking a promotion.

Recommendations on LinkedIn are very much like letters of referral. And the neat thing is, you can give recommendations as well as receive them. In fact, giving recommendations is the best way to begin.

As you are reviewing your initial first-degree network, there will be people you are well acquainted with. You know their work ethic and their capabilities. Perhaps you worked on a project together in college, or you were coworkers at your last company. Choose the ones you feel the best about and take the time to write a few recommendations.

# RECOMMENDATION BASICS

Keep all recommendations short—only a paragraph or two will suffice—and take care to see that it's professionally worded. Think of how you would want one to come back to you. This can be sent from either your home page or from your profile page.

You are prompted to indicate if you are a colleague, a service provider, or a business partner. The latter essentially means neither of the other two. (Obviously you have not been a real "business partner" with everyone for whom you are writing a recommendation.) From there you are asked to further clarify the relationship, followed by the space where the actual recommendation will be written.

That recipient may be very thankful for the recommendation, but would like it to be tweaked somewhat. It could come back to you with a note saying "Request Replacement." At which time you can connect with that person and see what can be added or adjusted. This is a helpful step because the recipient has no way of editing or changing it. They do, however, have the choice of whether or not to display what you've sent. The best remedy for making the recommendation as precise as possible the first time is to contact the person ahead of time and ask what specific details she might want added. If she is already building her personal brand, she may want you to address the strong points that are emphasized in her brand.

The key is to be specific. Address not only the recipient's abilities, but her personal attributes as well (make her seem real and alive and not some statistic). Indicate if the two of you have met personally; if you have actually worked together; if you have used that person's services, why you would recommend her as an employee, coworker, project coordinator, service provider, or whatever is appropriate. Again, be as specific as possible.

## HOW TO REQUEST A RECOMMENDATION

The best way to receive recommendations is to ask for them after a job well done. It is important that you make the request close to the time of completion of your work so that details are fresh for your recommendation.

The second aspect is to write a recommendation for a connection when you have been the recipient of good work. This is also a way of building your network and establishing a stronger professional relationship.

Here is a sample request for recommendation that I recently used after speaking at an event.

---

Dear Cindy,

I enjoyed my time at the Nebraska Travel Conference last week. I am writing you to ask you for a brief recommendation regarding my presentation that I can include in my LinkedIn profile.

If you have any questions, let me know.
Thanks in advance for helping me out.

-April Kelly

---

Although on your LinkedIn site you can request as many as two hundred of your contacts for recommendations, you can filter and refine and narrow your search. At the outset it's best to only ask from those who can actually give you a quality recommendation. LinkedIn provides a default message (canned message if you will), but you can go in and change that and the subject text.

So if there are details you would like included in your recommendation, mention them just as you would when asking for a referral letter. And it's perfectly okay to ask for revisions when you do receive a response.

Try to have your recommendations cover a wide variety of contacts. For instance, if you have a dozen recommendations from the personnel at your last place of employment and only two or three from other sources, that gives an unbalanced look. Add in the customers you encountered in your most recent position, and perhaps those you've worked alongside at the place where you volunteer, all of which give you a more well-rounded profile.

The Recommendations area of LinkedIn is one of the best places to work at building your personal brand. Use it wisely.

## TAP INTO YOUR RECOMMENDATIONS ON YOUR NEXT JOB SEARCH

Recommendations is also a perfect place to showcase your marketability during the hiring process. When you are in the midst of the hiring process, this will be the time when you will be eternally grateful that you have been building your LinkedIn presence ahead of time. After all, you never know when you are going to need it.

Because you have already been hard at work building up a network of relationships, now you can send a specific email regarding recommendations that play up the qualifications needed for a certain position that you are applying for. Your email to your contacts can outline exactly what details are needed in the recommendations.

Here is an example:

---

Dear Jane,

I am writing to ask for a recommendation of my management work. I am currently applying for a training position and would appreciate references to the effectiveness of my sales training program.

I appreciate your consideration. Please contact me if you have questions or concerns. Thank you.

---

This will result in your having a power-packed online portfolio that will set you head and shoulders above all the other candidates for the position.

Invest your time and effort in the Recommendations area, where valuable tools are available to move your career ahead.

Once you're comfortable with the Recommendations section of LinkedIn, it's time to really dive into what the site has to offer by getting involved in groups.

# 10. $\mathcal{L}$inkedIn Groups

**A**nother highly effective way to become known and recognized on the LinkedIn site is to join groups of like-minded people. You can join groups that are associated with your alumni, business interests, the company where you work, various industries, charities, and special interest groups. LinkedIn provides a directory of groups from which to choose. Fair warning: there are thousands of them.

Being a member of a variety of groups further allows you to expand your network. Once you are inside a group, you can now contact these members directly and view their profiles. You can do this even if they are not within your own personal network. This is one of the only areas of the website where you can interact with people you do not know.

Think of how much more expansive your reach becomes within these groups and how you can continue to grow your personal brand. Add to that the added opportunities for you to be found by those outside your network.

One way in which you can become proactive in the group you have joined is to start or join in Discussions. Be courteous enough to keep your comments on the subject at hand and never use such opportunities to promote yourself. If you take part in an ongoing discussion and add value to it, and if your appearance there occurs on a regular basis, you will begin to be noticed without having to toot your own horn. You develop yourself as a subject matter expert, which can prove to be important to other people in the industry. This is another strong branding attribute.

Every group bears a distinctive logo, so once you join a group, you can show that group logo on your profile page. Use common sense in this area. Although a few logos will show the fields in which you have an interest, too many logos will only clutter the page and obscure the message you want to give out. I recommend having no more than ten group logos.

## START AND GROW
## YOUR OWN GROUP

If you have a passion in a certain area and you don't find a group that fits your particular need, you may want to start up your own group. Or perhaps you are a member of an organization or group of professionals and you feel this would be the best place to find common ground for starting a new LinkedIn group.

Give a good deal of thought before taking this step because it will mean spending time in maintaining the membership and overseeing what goes on within the group. If you're not sure you can afford that time, don't start a group in the first place.

To begin a group you will need to create a catchy name and a distinctive logo and then decide in which category it will best fit. Keep in mind that LinkedIn will require you to submit your list of members. The LinkedIn staff then reviews the group and your contacts. Only then will they notify you if they will be adding your group to their list of groups.

If you set your group up well and let other like-minded people know about it, you will be found. You will want to pay particular attention to the keywords you use in the group description. You want compatible people who are searching a specific industry or interest to find your group in their search.

Now instead of simply being a member, you own your own group, and all who join have the option of placing your logo on their profile page. Visitors to their profile pages will see your logo—yet one more example of the potential of incredible viral growth of your network.

With the power of group discussions and news sharing, LinkedIn users have more and more platforms from which to herald their personal brands.

## COMPANY GROUPS

In addition to user groups, you will also find company groups within LinkedIn. Any and all current employees can be members of the group. It is becoming increasingly popular for big companies to vie for positions on LinkedIn to demonstrate their willingness to be visible and to allow more online interaction among their personnel.

If your company is not presently represented in an online LinkedIn group, you might want to be the one who sets things in motion to organize one. Usually the human resource or marketing department will oversee this type of activity for a business. In the event that an employee no longer works for a company, the company group manager is responsible for maintaining the integrity of the employees listed.

In addition to basic networking, companies are starting to use LinkedIn's Corporate Solutions and using LinkedIn to post jobs and locate viable candidates for open positions. Therefore, you want to be findable.

Likewise, job searching is another reason why it's so important to be connected on LinkedIn where you can be found if you are currently in a job search. Think of how much easier it is to research any company you're interested in. You will be able to search out—among other things—company statistics, new hires, promotions, contacts, and jobs posted. Additionally, here's the place where you could begin to build relationships with a few of a company's current employees and learn more about the workplace setting.

While company groups and company profiles differ somewhat from the user groups, you will find a number of avenues in which you can continue to build your network and continue to develop your memorable personal brand.

Company groups allow for interaction among current employees of the company. Company profile pages give everyone on LinkedIn a flavor for the culture of the company. It also lists employees on LinkedIn. This can be interesting in that by reviewing the profile of an employee it might reveal additional details about the company and potential opportunities. The more popular employees are ones located in the HR department as they have a strong pulse on the hiring activities of the company. User groups are much more generic in nature and this allows you more room to interact and establish your presence.

The bottom line on the subject of groups is much like all other areas of LinkedIn. What are your goals, what do you have to offer, and how can you be as proactive as possible without spamming? Use discretion and wisdom to make groups work for you while at the same time you will add value in your own right.

Navigating LinkedIn can take a learning curve. You'll have plenty of questions. LinkedIn has answers. A vast storehouse of knowledge is available in the Answers section of LinkedIn, which is the subject of the next chapter.

## 11. The Right "Answer"

**H**ave you ever wished you could step into a "brain trust" and ask all the questions you wanted to about your specific area of expertise, or about the industry you are involved in?

With LinkedIn Answers you can, essentially, do that very thing. This is the location on the site where questions are asked and answered on a regular basis. And you can be the questioner, and you can respond with answers to others' questions too.

## TAPPING THE BRAIN TRUST

When you go to your home page and click on the Answers link, LinkedIn automatically reviews your profile and brings up questions that relate to your areas of interest. You'll also see any questions that you have recently asked and answers you've posted.

By browsing through the "New Questions from Your Network," you can see what people in your first-degree network are asking. Or you can run through the list of "This Week's Top Experts."

LinkedIn offers many ways to search for and to browse through questions on the site. The Answers home page offers sixteen categories, plus a wide range of sub-categories, making it convenient and easy for you to locate the section that is closely related to the topic in which you have an interest.

I have used this area extensively for help of all sorts. When I was writing my first book, I ran into a few weeks of mental blocks. The book was nearing completion and this was unacceptable. I posed the question in the Answers section by asking how other people have overcome writer's block. I had about a dozen responses within the first day, and several of the suggestions were very helpful.

In another situation, I had a question about a recent book I had read on the topic of tax codes. I asked the question in Answers regarding this book and a tax situation and was most surprised. Not only did I get an answer, I heard from the author of the book. What a help it was to talk to the source. Answers is a powerful tool.

# CONTACTS THROUGH ANSWERS

Answers can also work to create contacts. For instance, someone may be looking for a technical writer in a certain field of expertise. Here's the posted question: *Does anyone know a technical writer who can interpret architectural terms for a project report?*

You may be scanning the list and see that question. Perhaps you are that writer, or you know someone who is. Either way, you can help out in this situation. If you have an opportunity to recommend a professional and promote that person's business, you will instantly make a fast friend. Your response might be: *A colleague of mine from college may be a good fit, I have pasted the link to his LinkedIn profile below. Please take a look and if you are interested, I would be happy to do an introduction.* This can be done through an InMail (LinkedIn's internal email service) to both of the parties involved.

If you are looking for a particular answer, you may want to browse the existing answers before posting a question as the subject may have already been covered. In other words, you might see that another procurement director has asked the "brain trust" to share their experiences in working with a new supplier. No need for you to ask the question again. Just tap into the answers. As you browse you'll see that there are many different categories and subcategories to help you narrow your search.

The questions you post to your network can be seen by your second and third degree connections. LinkedIn limits the number of questions you can ask to ten per calendar month. However, there is no limit on the number of questions you can answer.

When asking a question, you can post it on the site and then additionally notify your first-degree network via email. Since not all your contacts are checking their LinkedIn site on a daily basis, it will serve you better to use the email option. This can be sent to contact up to two hundred members of your network.

If you excel in a certain skill or area of knowledge, you would benefit by answering questions in your chosen field on a regular basis. The person who asked the question has the option to rate the answers after the question has closed (after seven days). The higher your questions are rated, the more you become visible and known as an expert.

This rating by your peers is noted by LinkedIn as they give "expert" status to individuals with a high number of "best answer" votes. It's their way of rewarding those who add value to the site. When you have posted a question, you will want to do the same by rating those who take the time and effort to answer your questions.

## KEEP YOUR EXPERTISE MANAGEABLE

Because this Q&A area is so vast and because it can be a real time-eater, you may want to limit your involvement to monitoring one or two areas—especially at the outset. It's important to keep your participation within a manageable size. If you find an *expert* whose answers are helping you, follow him or her and track those answers on a regular basis.

At some point, you may want to make a contact and begin to build a relationship. Having such a pool of experts at your fingertips is of inestimable value both for growing your personal brand and for the future of your career.

## Answers Strategy

It's a good idea to create a strategy for getting the most out of LinkedIn Answers. Think of it first and foremost as a way to contribute and add value to those around you. Choose your category, or categories, and create a work plan to answer questions within those parameters on a daily basis. Or weekly at the very least. Avoid blatant self-promotion at all costs.

Answer questions with direct facts and your audience will recognize your wisdom and appreciate your resourcefulness. When asking questions, be sincere in your question and be sure to thank everyone who takes time to respond to your question.

If you have a blog or website that is related to the subject at hand, and if you feel either of those sites adds value to your answer, you are justified in adding that link in your answer. Again, it all comes back to using wisdom and discretion.

When you have asked a question and individuals take the time to log their answers, be sure to thank them. Common courtesies go a long way in cementing online relationships.

If you start now by answering a few questions a day, and asking one or two questions a month, think of how your number of contacts will explode over the next year. In addition, so will your storehouse of knowledge in your chosen subjects.

Your personal brand will have become that much more remarkable and distinctive, and you'll essentially be setting yourself up as an expert on the site. There is plenty of knowledge on the Internet these days, but when you can go to your LinkedIn group and find a person who can answer your question from firsthand experience, that is very valuable. You'll instantly have people to welcome into your network, and these will be meaningful contacts who joined your network because you were helping them—not because you were looking for a favor. These types of contacts are invaluable.

LinkedIn offers an amazing array of methods in which to run searches. The next chapter shows you the most successful ways to search.

## 12. Not Your *Normal* Search

Even the newest newcomer to using the Internet quickly learns how valuable an online search can be. Type in a few words on a Google search and you can access incredible volumes of information. It is amazing. People love it and use it extensively.

The same is true with LinkedIn, but even more so. In fact, they have taken the idea of search to a whole new level. There are limitless combinations of basic and advanced searches to assist you in making your way through the maze of thousands of LinkedIn subscribers.

Most visitors to the site begin by looking for someone—a particular person. Others may be searching for a general group of people, such as those involved in a certain charitable organization or members of a university organization, perhaps a fraternity or sorority. Still others may be searching for a particular skill such as public relations or website design. All of these types of searches and many more are possible through the LinkedIn search system.

## ACCESSING SPECIAL CRITERIA

When you are logged into the site, the basic search form appears on every page. The dropdown menu gives the choices. You can search for People, Jobs, or Answers. The default is for People because that's the most common search.

Although this was not always the case, LinkedIn now allows you to search the entire membership and not just contacts in your own network. The improvement has been a boon to all members because you now have access to so many more variations of connections.

As a new member, your first search is usually by name since you may be looking for someone you used to work with or once attended college with. Since there may be a number of people with the same name, the advanced search allows you to bring in added criteria such as the name of the company, or the name of the college, the person's title, areas of interest, or even a zip code or locale.

In the basic people search function, you will find a tab in the left margin listed as Interested In.

This tab has numerous selection criteria such as these:

- Reconnect
- Industry Experts
- Reference Check
- Deal Making Contacts
- Hiring Managers
- Potential Employees
- Consultants/Contractors
- Entrepreneurs

From these sub-areas you can get a general idea of just how vast the scope of a people search can be. But that is just the tip of the iceberg.

Under the Contact tab on the top navigation bar, you can search by Connections. You may want to search for connections at specific employers or in a specific part of the world. This search area will allow you to narrow the search.

Once you have come up with a search result, you can continue to refine the search in four different ways:

- By keyword relevance
- By degrees and recommendations
- By degrees away from you
- By number of connections

## LOCATING SUPER-CONNECTORS

Some LinkedIn members specifically search for those who are known as "super-connectors." The super-connectors are people who have hundreds or perhaps even thousands of connections and are known as LIONs (LinkedIn Open Networkers). Rather than concentrating on a small number of strong relationships, they opt for a large number of weaker relationships. Because of the "number of connections" option from the previous search list, these individuals are easy to find.

The idea behind the LIONs is that they never turn down a connection. It would be rare to get a rejection from a LION, so it's probably worth your time to reach out through LinkedIn. These super-connectors are the people to know because their ability to connect you with almost anyone goes beyond what you could ever dream of. Just remember that you will have to prove yourself before you will be able to take advantage of a LION's network. Just as if you're applying for a job, you've got to make yourself stand out, and having your personal brand solidified and in place is one way to do that, especially when you contact this LION for the first time.

No matter what your strategy, it only takes hooking up with a couple of super-connectors to give your network a huge jump-start.

If you are an entrepreneur and you're searching for a professional to contract a specific job—say to design a website or create a logo—you may want to search under "number of recommendations" in your network. You can be fairly confident that a professional with a high number of recommendations will be reputable and trustworthy.

## FURTHER REFINE THE SEARCH

Further complexities of the search will involve using these functions:

- Use quotation marks to follow an exact phrase (such as *"sales copywriter"* to narrow the search for someone who writes sales copy and eliminating candidates who write technical copy).

- Exclude terms from the list of key words by placing a minus sign (- or a hyphen) in front of the term (in the previous example, you might use *-technical* to eliminate technical writers).

- Further define using Boolean searches such as AND, OR, and NOT (such as *sales NOT automobile*). Using the example of a sales professional, you may use a search that says: *sales OR marketing AND houses NOT automobiles.* This would yield a search for home sales and marketing experts.

All of these are commonly used search tools that you can learn more about through search engines like Google. When coupled with LinkedIn's advanced tools, the tools allow you to continue to narrow down your search results.

# INTRODUCTIONS

There may be occasions when you want to take your search a step further. Possibly you may know the person you want to contact, but you'd like to have a more personal connection—an introduction, so to speak.

For instance, you have an interest in a certain company, but you know no key people there. Put out the word through your own network asking if anyone knows someone from that company who is in a key position. If a response comes back, you can ask that person to act as your intermediary to offer to make the introduction. Many people have connected to high-profile individuals in this very way. Once the introduction has been completed, make it a point to send a heartfelt thank you to the person who took the time and effort to make that introduction.

When you write your introduction request, make sure your message is clear and strongly worded so you are making the best impression. If you have several contacts who are all connected to the person you want to meet, consider which one would carry the most weight in relaying the request. Which one do you think would give the matter the attention needed?

Take care that you are not making too many introduction requests within a short time frame. Try to maintain a reciprocal relationship with all your contacts. Introduce people in your network to others as well. A little consideration goes a long way.

Sample wording for an introduction:

---

Dear Bill,

Hello. I am looking for an expert with a background in tax law to assist me with a new venture. I noticed you are connected to Susan Smith, and her professional credentials may be a match for my project.

I am writing to ask you to make an introduction. I appreciate your assistance and am happy to return the favor as needed.

Thank you again for your help.

Sincerely, April Kelly

---

## When You Become the Intermediary

In another scenario, it's possible that you have two individuals in your network who do not know one another. Because you know them both, their talents and abilities, you feel they would benefit from becoming acquainted. You can then serve as the intermediary and initiate the introduction.

Both of them will be grateful and you have just added to the value of your networking system.

Paying it forward in situations such as this will return to you threefold and positions you as a "go to" person in the future.

Here is a copy of an introduction I made between two of my connections:

---

Hello, Rebecca,

I wanted to take a moment to introduce you to Jack. Jack is a dear friend of mine with a dynamic professional background. I think there may be some interesting synergies with ABC Services, so I thought it would be beneficial to connect the two of you.

Please let me know if there is anything further I can do to help facilitate contact.

---

## YOU ARE ASKED TO MAKE AN INTRODUCTION

It could be that you are the one who has been asked to make an introduction for another person in your network. Will you or won't you follow through? Only you can make that decision, but you may want to base your decision on how well you know the person making the request. Do you actually know enough about your old college roommate to feel comfortable in setting up the introduction with the HR manager of your company? If not, you may want to hold off.

Always use discretion when making the decision to decline. You may want to say something like: "I just don't feel comfortable passing that request along" or "I'm not the right person to make that introduction because I'm just not that close to that VP." Perhaps you've read the request and feel it's not worded well, or it needs further clarification. You may be able to make a few suggestions for a revised version that will make the grade, after which you can follow through and actually make the introduction.

If you yourself are a high-profile individual in your own right, you may receive more requests than you can possibly handle both personally and professionally. Either you learn to be highly selective or you can become overwhelmed and the effectiveness of the networking diminishes.

The option to make and request introductions makes the LinkedIn experience even more valuable. Whenever you use these kinds of opportunities to reach out to those in your network, you are reminding your contacts you're still here, you're still in business, and you're still a person with whom it pays to be connected. In other words, your personal brand and your network are being strengthened.

## 13. People You May Know

Newcomers to LinkedIn may be a little surprised when they first log in to find a list of three names under the heading People You May Know. You have the option to pursue these contacts further or remove them from your home page altogether. From there you can request further additions to this list.

Is it magic? How does LinkedIn know other professionals you might want to know? Or even already know but are not yet connected with?

For some LinkedIn users, this feature is nothing but a nuisance. For others it seems to be indispensable. It all depends on your particular position and why you chose to use LinkedIn in the first place.

Actually, when used correctly, the People You May Know feature can be of great benefit to you and your expanding network. A name might appear on the list of someone you were acquainted with in the past but have completely forgotten about. Here's the chance to renew the relationship and reconnect.

One of the ways to assure that your People You May Know list is as relevant as possible is for you to see to it that your profile is detailed. The more information in your profile, the more connections LinkedIn can make. In other words, you can list prior companies where you were employed and add the positions held and titles as well. List schools, universities, organizations you belong to, charities you support, and hobbies you enjoy. Each of these categories will give additional keywords to match you with potential people you may know.

Just as with all other aspects of LinkedIn, the possibilities are endless. However, the network only works as well as you allow it to. Take advantage of the feature by investing a few minutes to follow up on the names that are of interest to you. And use the handy "delete" button for the rest.

Since LinkedIn is never a one-way street, every time you note that People You May Know box, take a moment to stop and consider how many LinkedIn sites that *your* name may be appearing on.

Again, it's yet another way in which LinkedIn is assisting you in your brand-building process.

As the LinkedIn site continues to grow and evolve, it is being used ever more frequently as a place to post jobs and find jobs—the subject of the next chapter.

# 14. Tap into the Gold Mine of Jobs and Hiring

**W**hen it comes to finding jobs online, LinkedIn is a veritable gold mine, and the many stories of professionals who have successfully used the site for that reason supply the proof.

The time to begin mining your network is now—not when you are already in need of a job. Your network foundation should be in place before job hunting becomes necessary. And it's because of the extraordinary networking features of LinkedIn that the job hunting section works so well.

Most professionals today are aware of the many job boards that are available. Sites such as Monster.com, Jobs.com, Careerbuilder.com, and Jobster.com have become increasingly popular in the past few years. And each one has it pros and cons. One of the biggest complaints heard is how impersonal these sites are and how difficult it is to actually get your information into the hands of the right people.

Some say they send their résumé and never hear anything back. It's as though their information goes into a black hole never to be heard of again. Others become disgruntled because an ad asking for a "Director of Marketing" or "Marketing Manager" turns out to be a multi-level marketing or MLM organization. And it's impossible to tell from the ad whether it's valid or bogus.

Complaints were also voiced regarding unwanted solicitations that came quickly on the heels of their listing on the job boards. Some of those emails came from recruiters and headhunters that had no real positions to fill, but contacted job seekers anyway.

This is not to say the job boards do not have successes. But when compared to the process offered by LinkedIn, they are much more difficult to navigate.

## LINKEDIN'S PROCESS

The Jobs and Hiring section on the LinkedIn site can be found by clicking on the Jobs link on the member home page. From here you can begin to browse in any number of different ways. You may begin by simply scanning through the most recent jobs listed.

All job listings are organized into five columns:
- Job title
- Company
- Location
- Date the job was posted
- Name of job poster

This is where LinkedIn and other job boards part company—the last column where the name of the job poster is revealed.

That individual who posted the position is a member of LinkedIn and also has a profile. You will see the number of recommendations he has received, who made them, and when. If the job poster is in your extended network, his name and degree of connection to you will be shown. And what's more, he is automatically sorted to the top of the list. This is an excellent way to get your foot in the door by mentioning your common connection.

If the poster is not in your network, there are still other alternatives if you wish to connect. The Jobs page will indicate how many connections you have in your network who are inside this particular hiring company. You can also see how many of them are friends of your connections. Now you have a pathway that clearly shows how you could possibly network closer and closer to that job.

If you have a connection with a friend close to a job that interests you, this is a perfect time to ask for an introduction to solicit feedback about the employment opportunity.

How different it would be if every job board allowed you to know who to talk to, or showed you the person you know who might be in a position to set up an introduction. Suddenly the job search would become personal again. You wouldn't feel like a hamster in a wheel, just making the rounds of the employment sites tossing your résumé into black holes.

Jobs can be searched for on your LinkedIn site by keyword, company, location, or job title as well. And similar to the people search, there are any number of ways to refine your search and narrow it down.

## APPLY ON SITE

If you happen to find a job that is of interest to you, you can apply for that position right there within the LinkedIn site. You'll have the option to create your professional cover letter, upload your résumé, and send it off. When you apply in this way, your LinkedIn profile is also sent to that job poster. (Now you understand more fully how vital it is to have a full and informative profile set up on your LinkedIn site. You also understand how beneficial it can be to have a number of high-quality recommendations from a wide variety of sources.)

However, you may not want to do any of this until, as I stated previously, you have networked your way closer to the company and the job poster. When you're able to fall back on a more personal relationship rather than just a vague mention of someone you both happen to have met once upon a time, you actually come to life in the eyes of the job poster.

# HIRING AND RECRUITING

For obvious reasons, LinkedIn is as popular with recruiters as it is with job hunters. Instead of sorting through dozens and dozens of résumés, the recruiter has a network to select a worthy candidate from. Many recruiters begin by distributing a new job listing to their connections within the network first asking for their help in the hiring process.

As with those who are hunting for jobs, the criteria for the People search allows you to search in various ways. You may want to begin with keywords and position title and narrow the search from there.

Most recruiters will say that searching for professionals through LinkedIn saves them hours of work. It takes only a few minutes to review a profile. If the talent looks promising but more information is required, the connections are there to provide the needed details.

Although the job boards still have their place—and people are obviously still using them—LinkedIn exceeds them all in its effectiveness, simplicity, and ease of use for both those who are looking for a job and those who are recruiting. Now let's dig deeper inside the advanced techniques available to you on LinkedIn.

# 15. Applications – LinkedIn's Advanced Techniques

The LinkedIn experience is an ever-evolving and ever-growing experience. Just like going to the beach, you can stay in the shallows, or grab your boogie board and launch out into the deep water. Or maintain a position somewhere in the middle. The same with your LinkedIn site experience. It's all up to you—whatever rounds out your need in building your personal brand.

Because there are those who want to go deeper and deeper, LinkedIn provides a number of applications. No one needs to use them all or use them all at once. The best plan is to move slowly but steadily by incorporating one at a time, wait to see how the venture fares, then go on to the next. Once you become familiar with each advanced technique, you will further understand which ones best suit your particular needs. Let's start with the Polls application.

# POLLS

At first glance the idea of adding a poll to your LinkedIn site may seem somewhat frivolous. However, it can be a way to tap into the wisdom and knowledge of scores, if not hundreds, of professionals. Its scope is as vast as your imagination.

A poll could provide answers to your research questions. Or it could give you feedback of opinions affecting a marketing decision. Your target audience can be your own network, or you can seek selected professionals in a certain industry. LinkedIn then steps in and assists by analyzing the results. You will know how such things as seniority, company size, job function, age, and gender affect the responses you receive.

The first step is to go to the Applications area of the LinkedIn website and look for the Polls application. After you click on the Polls feature, you will notice a button that will allow you to create a new poll. Here you will see the boxes where you write out the questions and then add your selection of possible answers.

After you are done constructing your poll, you will be able to send your poll to any of your connections as well as broadcast it through Twitter if you have added your Twitter ID to your LinkedIn profile. You can also add it to a status update to attract more attention to your poll. As a final step, your poll will show up in the LinkedIn poll listings so other LinkedIn members can respond.

Responding is, of course, optional, but most people who receive a poll will take the two seconds to respond.

The poll results will be shown in a graph style that allows easy analyzing of the answers. You can also browse the results by segments to find out how each group answered and the percentages of each.

Here is a sample from one of my polls (Source: LinkedIn, April Kelly):

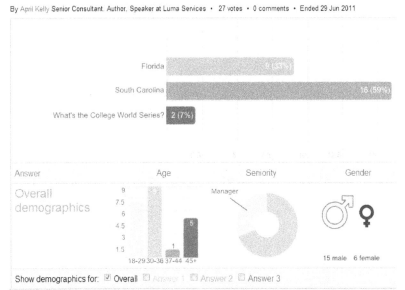

## Who will win the College World Series?
By April Kelly Senior Consultant. Author, Speaker at Luma Services • 27 votes • 0 comments • Ended 29 Jun 2011

The Poll application will not only aid you in mining entire storehouses of facts and information, it also serves as yet another way to get your name and your presence out to many others in the growing LinkedIn family—whether that means only your network or expanding out from there.

Your name and your personal brand will be making an impact. What an excellent way to create your own type of public relations campaign.

## EVENTS

Closely related to the Poll application is the Event application. If you are involved in presenting workshops, seminars, or speaking at conferences, don't fail to use this feature to promote these events.

Simply click on Applications on the left of your profile and select Events. Once you click on that, you are able to post an event. It doesn't take a lot of savvy to grasp the far-reaching effects of this application. Again, you are tapping into a public relations opportunity that is quick, easy, and free.

On the flip side, you may be following key people. Watching their events postings can help you to perhaps attend one of their events and meet them personally. Or the description of their presentation could help you learn more about the extent of their expertise in a certain area.

Whether you are posting your own events or following the events of others, you will benefit in a big way from this application.

Here is a sample event (Source: LinkedIn, April Kelly):

## READING LIST

What are the professionals in your industry reading? What are your colleagues reading? What are you reading? All of these answers and more can be shared in the Reading List application. This particular application is powered by amazon.

After clicking on the Application box on the left of your Profile page, scroll down to Reading List. Here you can add what you are planning to read, what you have read in the past, and what you're reading now.

This application allows you to watch the reading list of selected people in your network. It also allows you to search out who is reading your favorite book. This can serve as a unique way to make new connections. A shared appreciation of a particular book helps you jump start an online conversation.

If professionals in your field are recommending a certain title, what a valuable way to learn about books you might not have otherwise ever heard of.

Because the Reading List application connects you with amazon.com, you have now opened up an opportunity to write book reviews. Writing reviews provides yet another avenue for you to make your personality and your presence known. This will work especially well if you review books that are relative to your industry. It provides an effective, noninvasive platform for you.

## MY TRAVEL

The My Travel (or Tripit) Application is an adventurous application. If you are planning a business trip and it is featured through Tripit, it's possible you could connect with others in your network who live in the area. Or you might learn of others in your network who are also attending the same function. Knowing this information ahead of time allows you to correlate your agendas and set up meetings that might not have otherwise happened.

As soon as your trip is posted (either on your home page or your profile or both), LinkedIn will show who will be close to you as you travel. This allows not only for business connections but possibly social interaction, giving you a chance to meet members of your online network face to face.

As with other features of LinkedIn, Tripit allows for two-way action. You will be posting the details of your trips, while at the same time you can preview the travels of your colleagues and other network members. This extension of the networking process will help you make the most of every trip you take and could result in a critical connection that could change your future for the better. (A word of caution: Just like autoresponders for email saying you're out of the office wave a red flag that you're traveling, enterprising burglars can take advantage of information about your travels with Tripit. Be cautious.)

# WORDPRESS

LinkedIn offers a feature to connect your WordPress blog with your LinkedIn site. Once this process is completed, you have choices on how to filter the posts with special LinkedIn tags. If you have a WordPress gravatar (global avatar), this can be added as well to give your blog added personality. Think of a gravatar as an online icon that represents you online. It is usually a photo or picture you develop and attach to your online work. Your blog updates will then be sent instantly to your network.

Because blogging is an external feature with regard to LinkedIn and personal branding, look for more discussion on this subject in more detail in Part Three of this book. Suffice it to say at this point that if you do maintain a blog, LinkedIn has made it super simple and easy to integrate it with your LinkedIn site.

# UNCONVENTIONAL LINKEDIN USES

Innovative, creative LinkedIn members have come up with any number of more unconventional uses for networking through the site. I'll just mention a couple here to give an idea of how extensive and far reaching LinkedIn can actually be.

Let's say you are a member of, or an officer in, an active nonprofit organization. At times that organization may be looking for a board member. By using their list of qualifications and parameters for such a position, a search can be executed through LinkedIn to locate potential candidates. And, as has been demonstrated, that candidate could be in the second or third degree and may require an intermediary to set up the introduction. Either way, the LinkedIn network will prove of high value for any nonprofit.

The network could also provide potential supporters for a specific fund-raising event. Key people could be tapped for helping with donations, or even with providing the facilities needed for the event.

I am also familiar with entrepreneurs seeking venture capital and locating their investors with the LinkedIn network. In an economy where money is tight, capital is difficult to come by.

That may be true in a broad sense, but remember you are now in a special select group. You will find there are venture capital people within the LinkedIn network who are more than ready to look at a possible venture within their particular industry.

Perhaps these examples will set your creative juices flowing to come up with even more unconventional ways to put this massive network to work for you.

As you have learned through this section of the book, LinkedIn can play a vital role in the growth and development of your personal brand. Although it should not be the only resource you use—nor should any other media—still you can see how expansive the reach of LinkedIn can be when used correctly. It takes time and a concerted effort to build and maintain an effective network. It's an ongoing process. Once you become active on LinkedIn, you'll see how all your other brand-building tools can seamlessly interact and blend together.

Part Three explores even more tools available to you as you make Me, Inc., a more memorable and marketable company.

## New Ingredients

As you begin developing your brand and utilizing the online tools, there is a good chance that the tools will improve and change. The current suite of social media tools have been developed by innovative product teams. These teams are also constantly looking to improve the user experience.

Be on the lookout for new ingredients or an improved tool within the site. I am sharing this information with you because some of the content you read in this book may also evolve and change in tandem with the referenced tools.

To remain up-to-date with the latest modifications, you can read a company blog and set a news alert, which can help track current events with a social media tool. In addition, when a feature is removed from a website, it may signal that a new and improved version is on the way.

When I am looking for the most current information on a website, I refer to the following areas:

LinkedIn: LinkedIn Blog and Help Center

Twitter: Help Center

Facebook: Help Center

Pinterest: Help Center

# Part Three
## Dishing Up Your
## Personal Brand

## 16. *M*odern Branding for Mature Professionals

**A**re you convinced by now that you not only need your own personal brand, but need to know what that brand is (by using your personal brand statement) and what image you want to portray to make yourself stand out from the crowd?

Imagine brands like "Got Milk?" being left on a shelf. Instead it was coupled with compelling people and ad space. The signature white moustache added a defining element. Your brand has the same potential.

You know how you want to exhibit your unique individuality in a way that not only enhances your career, but your entire life. Here's more. This final part of the book discusses a variety of different ways that a personal brand can be created, built, and nurtured. Some of these methods are online, others are offline, but all can be highly effective.

My brand includes these attributes: Author, Artist, and Gratitude Leader. My message has evolved into this:

> Communication and Organizational Consultant who honors the need to hire and retain employees who are fully engaged, empowered, and eager to make a positive difference in the lives of their coworkers and customers.

Now the next step is to actually take your brand and make it into a reality. Having an idea for a brand is not the same as circulating that brand and actually getting it out there. Your personal brand does not begin to live until you've moved it out of your mind and into the world where it will get results.

Think about your brand as the answer to the question: *What do you do?* Other people call this an elevator speech. Does your brand fulfill this role?

## Something to Wrap Your Noodle Around

Now it's time for you to express your personal brand by tinkering with your elevator speech.

What do you do?

How do you do it?

Can others understand what you do if you have twenty seconds to tell them?

# WHERE TO PROMOTE YOUR BRAND

LinkedIn is probably one of the best spaces for promoting your personal brand. Professionals are going to the site in droves to find other professionals they can connect with on projects and in other areas. LinkedIn is the place to find profiles of people you can work with. This is why you can't afford not to utilize all the tools LinkedIn has to offer.

Also having your own website is a vital part of advertising your brand, as is writing articles in your niche and blogging about it.

# BUILDING YOUR NICHE

One of the mistakes many people make when they set about creating their personal brand is forgetting about their niche. One way to set yourself apart from others is by finding and utilizing your niche. For instance, to say my niche is "leadership" is somewhat vague. Adding a clarification such as gratitude leader defines a specific niche, and this is where my brand takes root.

There may be several or even thousands of people who have the same name as you, but they all don't have the same interests or strengths as you. This is what makes you different, and advertising that niche as part of your personal brand is essential. No one else named April Kelly bills herself as a gratitude leader.

Your brand message should definitely tie in with your niche in some way. When people see your message, they should immediately think of someone who is an expert in your particular field. This will help establish you as the Jane Doe who is a marketing guru rather than the Jane Doe who is an incredible painter.

One of the biggest barriers to personal branding is the feeling that it's something you simply don't have to do. You might make the excuse that you are too old or too young. You might think you can take a break from branding just to catch a breath and enjoy the job you currently have. However, there is no better time to begin building your brand now, and this is something that will be a lifelong process.

Be vigilant in your brand building and think not just about your past, present, or future, but also about what could be. You're never too old to brand yourself, and you will never reach a point where keeping up your brand is unimportant.

Coca-Cola, for example, has been around since 1886, and the company has never let up on its brand. Any time they attempted to make a major change, there was great public backlash, as can be expected with a product that is branded so well. In 1985 when Coke tried to change the formula of the soft drink by creating New Coke, the public was so outraged that the company ended up changing back to a variation of the old recipe just a few months later.

Coke had succeeded in branding itself so well that consumers refused to have it any other way. Just the insertion of the word *new* into their brand indicated that something was different, and in spite of taste tests that showed the average consumer preferred the taste of New Coke over the original, the public as a whole refused to accept any other brand except for the original Coke. Today Coke continues to brand itself under the Coca-Cola Classic name, and the company hasn't tried to change the recipe since.

This is the success you should shoot for with your personal branding. When you have branded yourself so well that people will accept no substitute, you know that the message about who you are has gotten across. Companies may change their slogan from time to time, and you should also change yours periodically, but the brand is something that should never change.

Your brand is your identity, and if you've established it properly, no one will let you change it.

## ACT YOUR AGE

Another issue dealing with the timing of branding has to do directly with your age. It can be difficult to develop a new brand for yourself amidst all these twenty-something freshly graduated professionals. On the other hand, your brand shouldn't be exactly the same as it was when you first graduated from college. Your brand identity shouldn't change, but the way you present that brand should. For Baby Boomers and Gen Xers, the key is to take the brand you have created throughout the years and simply update it for your higher maturity level.

Of course it may seem overwhelming because sometimes coming up with a personal brand feels as if you have to reinvent yourself, but this certainly is not the case. You're not reinventing yourself, but, rather, you're reinventing the way you present yourself to the world. Instead of changing who you are, you're changing the way you communicate yourself to the world.

## BRANDING FOR THE FIRST TIME

Baby Boomers or Gen Xers who never quite developed their personal brand may find it difficult to do so now, simply because you don't know where to start. However, the key to developing a new brand is to look at where you've been and figure out how to use that to your advantage. There's no need to reinvent the wheel here. All you're doing is viewing the path of your life and seeing how far you have come. You'll pick up clues along the way that will indicate the brand you have built without even realizing it.

Let's start with the very first job you had. Some people tend to skip over those summer or part-time jobs they held as a teenager, but if you did work as a young person, it's still important to consider these positions because they can say a lot about you. Often it's not necessarily the position itself but the way you performed in that position.

So whenever your first job was, think about what the job was, whether you liked it, and what your coworkers said about you. Do the same for every job you've ever had, moving through the timeline of your life. You'll begin to see some patterns emerge. First, you'll probably notice some similarities in the types of jobs you had. For example, if you often took a leadership role, even as a young person, you may eventually see yourself in a major management position. You also may notice jobs that all fall within the same industry.

Considering the way your coworkers saw you should also help you realize a pattern. Of course the key here is to take what they all said and look at it in a positive light, even if they didn't do so. Let's face it. Not everyone gets along in the workplace, but everyone does have something to say about their coworkers. Were you the bossy one who always made sure things got done? Were you the shy, quiet one who always kept to herself? All of these character traits go into creating who you are, and they have all ended up as part of your personal brand.

This is only the first part of your brand. You still need to come up with a catchy way to "package" yourself. But it all starts with knowing yourself and understanding how others view you as a person and as a coworker or boss.

# UPDATING YOUR BRAND

As a Baby Boomer or a Gen Xer, the most interesting step may be updating your brand. Even if you are creating a personal brand for the very first time, chances are it will need an update from time to time as it keeps pace with your career track. You start forging your working personality from a very young age, but that personality changes throughout the years as you mature. Even your current job may not say everything there is to say about you.

Now is the time to incorporate those things that may not be as apparent about you. If you're the shy, quiet type, your bosses, coworkers, or employees probably don't know much about you. When you begin to build your personal brand, this is the time to consider what you want others to say about you. For example, women who have always wanted to be a leader in a more overt way can find certain strings to pull out of their jobs. Leaders tend to have very specific characteristics, even when they are the shy, quiet types.

There are many different types of leaders. Some lead by example, while others are the more outgoing, demanding type. When you're building a brand around leadership, you've got to get creative with the way you view your previous jobs. Look for the ways you led others, even if they didn't see these techniques as leadership skills. Your personal brand can say anything you want it to say about yourself. It's all a matter of something the media world calls "spin."

Personal branding gives you the option to spin what others say about you the way you want it to go. It's sort of looking at the glass as half full instead of half empty. Even the traits others find to be annoying at times can usually be made into something good, especially when you focus on the positive side of it.

So now the only question is how to go about branding yourself. By this point you should have plenty of ideas about what you want your brand to say about you, but you probably aren't sure yet how to go about creating your brand. The entire process starts with the traits you already possess, but it isn't finished until you have a polished package that comes complete with a brand message and an image that will be remembered.

The very first step in your quest for personal branding is learning how to communicate yourself to the world.

## 17. Communication

Communication is an important part of creating a personal brand. The way you communicate yourself to the world is personal and unique. And just as the corporate environment is changing rapidly, so are the ways we communicate. In order to communicate your personal brand successfully, you've got to be in step with the times. That means not only being in sync with the vehicles of current communication, but also with the words that are in common use today.

Think about the term *business casual*. It is predominant in business and yet ask people to define it and you will get a vast array of responses with little consistency. This term can create confusion unless appropriately communicated, which would include a definition of the term to ensure clarity along with an example of just exactly what you might expect a man and a woman to wear to the workplace.

Another area impacted is the written word. How many emails do you receive in contrast to physical letters? Communication form has changed as well as content.

While it's true that you wouldn't use casual language in business correspondence, it's also true that the words you do use should be up-to-date and geared toward the audience you actually want to reach.

There are many different ways to communicate. Different cultures communicate differently, and even within cultures, you find varying styles of communication. Children communicate with each other one way and with adults another way. One of the biggest gaps is the difference between how men and women communicate. Then of course you have the differences between how men and women communicate in various social spheres, including the workplace. Men talk to men a certain way, they talk to women another way, and the same for women.

For the purposes of this book, let's look specifically at how women interact and communicate.

One of the biggest issues for women, especially Baby Boomers and even some early Gen Xers, is feeling like a woman in a man's world. Traditionally the world of business was a man's home, but today corporate America is not discriminatory. Both men and women make incredible leaders in the business world, but the way they lead is different and dependent largely on the way they communicate.

# COMMUNICATING
# YOUR PERSONAL BRAND

The way you communicate your personal brand says a lot about you. Communicating boldly shows that you are a bold person, for example. The key is to communicate in such a way that your target audience understands who you are and what you are about. In some cases, this may mean communicating in a way that is universally understood by both men and women.

Sometimes men and women do have trouble communicating with each other because it seems as if we speak different languages; for example, women tend to be more verbal in their communication styles. Men, on the other hand, may express themselves through their deeds and actions. There are ways to overcome these differences and communicate your personal brand message in a way that both men and women understand.

Women tend to be talkers, while men tend to get straight to the point. Women prefer to talk their problems out, while men are doers instead. Women enjoy a more personal touch in life, while men just want to know what the point of everything is so they can move on and get crackin' with the next action. When women get together, they want to have coffee and chat, but when men get together, they want the gathering to be around some sort of action, like fishing, attending a ball game, or doing some other activity.

In short, women are the real communicators, while men are more action-oriented in what they do. Women tend to have a bit more finesse in the way they communicate, but they also tend to be more emotional.

Emotions can be both a positive and a negative thing when it comes to communicating, but the good news with personal branding is that it is a very controlled environment in the area of communication. Emotions can and should be kept to a minimum when creating a personal brand. You have plenty of time to figure out what you want to express about yourself, so there's no need to rush. But the problem truly lies in finding the words to describe yourself in precisely the way you want to present yourself.

## Practice Communicating Your Personal Brand

Personal branding is largely about communicating yourself to the world, and it's impossible to know how successful your efforts will be without the input of others. This is why I suggest taking part in a MasterMind group or even creating your own dream team of people you can turn to.

A MasterMind group is essentially a collection of like-minded individuals who can weigh in on your ideas. In turn, you'll tell them what you think of their ideas. When you're trying to figure out the best way to communicate your brand to others, it's essential that you have a MasterMind group or dream team to give you input on whether you're evoking the right message in the best way.

If you don't have a MasterMind group or a dream team set up, you probably do have a close group of friends that you already trust.

Write about two or three different versions of your personal branding statement and then share them with the group (refer to chapter 3 for a refresher and some examples). Your personal brand statement should consist of only one sentence—two at the most—and should incorporate your unique values that you have identified.

You'll be amazed at what impression they take away from those messages and also the insight they can provide on these phrases. If they know you well enough, they should be able to tell you whether what you have written accurately reflects you, your expertise, and your personality well enough. You might even consider asking the other people in your MasterMind group to come up with a phrase or two that they think describes you. Sometimes seeing yourself through the eyes of others is just what you need to get a fresh perspective on yourself and the "professional you" everyone else sees.

# CREATING YOUR DREAM TEAM

Creating your brand and then living it every single day can seem like an impossible task. You've got to be on your toes at every moment, but it can certainly be done, especially when you have help.

As a professional, you need your own personal dream team. You can't expect to be able to go it alone without anyone else watching out for you. But the good news is that you can reciprocate and create some incredible exchange relationships by also watching out for the other people on your dream team. Sometimes it's easier to see things that are happening to other people than to yourself because issues can be right under your nose but impossible for you to see on your own. This is why you need a dream team of people you trust, respect, and can exchange with.

Think of your dream team as an extension of the "brain trust" you create on LinkedIn. I've talked about how you can grow your online network by making connections and by asking and answering questions within your field on LinkedIn. But even more important than your online network is your offline network. It should include people you trust and who can trust you as well.

For many women in particular, the idea of trusting someone else with her brand and identity seems preposterous. Working with other women can be the best experience in life or the worst one. Women can be kind and understanding, or they can be predatory and back-stabbing. This makes it very difficult to trust anyone because you never know what you're going to get until it is too late. Many women get where they are in the world by limiting their trust in other people, especially in other women. But this is the wrong way to look at things.

Your dream team can be made up of both men and women. It should be a trusted group of professionals you can exchange with. The point of a MasterMind group is to meet regularly and bounce ideas off each other. You can also help each other solve problems.

Try to get people from various industries but who are in about the same place of life as you. By comparing experiences and sharing together, you'll make each other stronger. Where one of you has gone through a particular situation, another has not, so he or she will need some guidance from the group. Each member of the group has a unique perspective to share with the others, and this group of perspectives is very valuable.

MasterMind groups have been in existence for centuries. Some of the most well-known MasterMind groups have included people like Thomas Edison, Henry Ford, and Bill Clinton. Most professionals use a MasterMind group, whether they call it by that term or not.

Besides sharing experiences, your MasterMind group will also give you some amazing ideas to help with your personal branding mission. They'll tell you about what they've tried that did and didn't work, and you can share your experiences as well. Additionally, you'll each be watching out for one another. If something sounds like a bad idea, one of your group members will tell you about it. When someone in your group sees something about you that isn't good, she'll tell you about it so that you can do some damage control. You can also find guidance on how to handle issues with your personal brand message, including any damage that has been done to it.

Having a MasterMind group also creates a unique segment within your network. It's one of the best ways to bring personal branding and networking together because you'll have your own personal network of people to not only help you with referrals and job opportunities, but also to give you ideas on how to freshen up your personal brand image.

A MasterMind group can also help you with your goal setting and keep you on track for what you want to accomplish. Anyone can set goals, but not everyone can meet their goals because they aren't able to manage themselves properly. It takes a lot of self-control to consistently meet your goals, but a MasterMind group can help take some of the mystery out of this process.

Accountability is a major part of goal setting, and if you're setting goals in your own life, who are you accountable to? Most people are more accountable to other people, so they put themselves last and end up forgetting all about their own goals, but when your MasterMind group is holding you accountable for your own goals, suddenly they become much more than just your goals. You'll realize immediately that your MasterMind group members are going to hold you to those goals, even if you sometimes don't feel important enough to place yourself on your own to-do list.

The group is usually made up of three to six people, and these are colleagues whom you trust. You can meet as frequently as needed. I recommend meeting at least monthly. Meetings can be done in person or via conference call. The group will help decide what works best for everyone. This is not a tips group for sales leads. This is a group of individuals with whom you share similar interests on some level; however, the members usually bring different skill sets that complement each other.

A typical group, for example, might form when a business owner invites includes her attorney and a friend in marketing and advertising. And one of these people brings in an accountant and a real estate sales professional and another small business owner.

## COMMUNICATING WITH OTHER STYLES

As you continue your search for the perfect personal brand message, just keep these different communication styles in mind. Your brand should be just a small sample of your own communication style, but it should be done in such a way that it speaks to people with other styles of communication. Men and women should both be able to take something away from your message, although exactly what they take away may be slightly different, and that's okay as long as the multiple messages you're sending out are all accurate.

In order to create a personal brand message that reaches both men and women successfully, it needs to be straight and to the point while also leaving just a hint of mystery to it. You don't want people to have to guess what you're all about, but it's always better to evoke just a bit of a question or thought into someone else's mind because they are more likely to remember it. When something you say sparks an idea in someone else's mind, he or she will remember you for it, guaranteed.

## 18. Personal Positioning

**O**ne of the earliest books to talk about personal branding was *Positioning: The Battle for Your Mind* by Al Ries and Jack Trout. Most of the book is about branding and especially positioning a company's brand, but the tips can be applied to you as a person as well—the Me, Inc. chapter of the book focuses entirely on positioning and how to apply the ideas to yourself.

Positioning is, in essence, slightly different than personal branding, however. Positioning assumes that you already have a brand in place and are able to position it appropriately in ways that will bring you success. It is still an important part of branding though because, without positioning, your personal brand can't exist. These two concepts need each other.

# PUT YOUR BRAND OUT THERE

It does you no good to have a personal brand and not put it out there where it can be found. We've dealt a lot with how to put your brand online, but there is a lot more to it than that. Branding also includes your day-to-day behavior and simply living your brand every single day. In other words, do your actions support your brand? An obvious example would be if you are an image consultant, are you walking out the door in a coordinated outfit?

But positioning is essentially making sure that you put your brand in a place where the right people will see it. For example, if you were advertising a new baby product, would you put it in a place where only men would see it? Probably not. You want new mothers. Dads might have some influence over the baby products purchased, but not nearly as much as the new moms would have.

You really have to think things through and determine your target market before you begin tossing anything out there. Not going about this strategically is like wearing a blindfold and throwing darts at the board. The only way you'll hit the bull's-eye is if you know who you are and where you're going (your personal brand!) and also the kinds of people you can benefit and benefit from.

You can network until you're blue in the face, but if you're not networking with the right kinds of people, then it will do you no good. You may discover one day that the groups you belong in have not been making you many profits. Perhaps you ended up in a crowd with people who do not need your services; consequently, you don't get connected to potential new clients. You've got to reposition your brand so that you can find these new clients. They're out there somewhere, and they probably won't come looking for you. You've got to go looking for them, and the only way to do this is by positioning yourself so that they can find you.

If you've been coming up with too many dead ends in your professional life, think for a moment about your position. What kinds of people do you come into contact regularly with because of the network you have right now? If you could change your network, how would you change it?

Your network increases in value when you're able to find people you can exchange with. It's never healthy to be in a network where you're a giver and everyone else is a taker. It's also not healthy to continually be taking from someone in your network. You need an even exchange over time, and if you're not finding that in your current network, then it's time to reposition yourself.

One woman I know, for example, was invited to a networking group of women. She attended weekly, brought lunch during her week to bring, shared her business plan about her communication and publication venture, and genuinely asked the other attendees about their work. She finally realized, she told me, that these women were not her market. She was a home-based business. The others were in real estate or insurance or banking. They had nothing in common with her and were not her market. She politely excused herself from further meetings.

Another person—a health insurance broker—found himself at a networking event held by a local business consortium. During the event, he was the only attendee asking questions of the speakers. Others turned to him for information on their small business insurance plans. Again, this was not a good fit for him because he wasn't going to get any business out of this. The balance or exchange of information was one-sided and not in his favor.

Your time is important. Don't spend more time in groups that don't work for you, even if the coffee talk is interesting and the sweet rolls are tasty.

You have control over your network. If you feel the need to change your network, then do so. Your brand will just fall flat if you aren't positioning yourself in a place where the right people will hear about you.

## 19. To Blog or Not to Blog

**B**eing able to communicate and position your brand are just the first steps in creating your public persona. The next is actively using the tools that are available to you as part of your branding campaign.

LinkedIn is an excellent tool for personal branding and networking, but there are other tools you should have in your toolbox as well, and these all require that you be able to communicate your brand loudly and clearly.

One of the first things you should be doing to establish your brand is to set yourself up as an expert in the field, and the easiest way to do this is to start with creating your own blog.

# WEB LOG = BLOG

For Baby Boomers, this term certainly does seem like a foreign one. At one time a blog was simply a few computer-savvy people writing diary-like entries on blog sites and sharing them with a few friends, but that certainly isn't the case anymore. Today it's the simplest way to show others that you are an authority in your industry. The term blog is derived from a blending of the two words Web and log. The early bloggers were simply logging their thoughts on the Web. Most of it was of little consequence and of little interest to anyone except a select few.

Fast forward a few years to the present when there are hundreds of thousands of new blogs created each day. Today even large companies maintain their own blogs, as do business executives, celebrities, and just about every other person you know. Can a blog be of help in this journey you're on to create your personal brand? If done correctly, it could be an enormous help. But it's good to know first of all what constitutes a quality blog and what is required to create one.

If you did the basic foundational work suggested in Part One of the book, now you know who you are, what you want, and where you're going. Based on that, you know what image you want portrayed and, thereby, the basis for a blog. All of these aspects will come into play as you make decisions as to the style, tone, content, and even the color patterns that will be used. The great advantage of a blog is that it will be totally and uniquely you!

## Blog Host

Blogging is online content provided by you. The content resides online and is accessible by anyone else online around the globe. To establish your blog, you will need to select a blog host. A blog host is a company that provides the space on their servers to store and support your blog. The most popular and well-known services are WordPress, TypePad, Movable Type, and Blogger. Each one has its own merits. You will want to review each blog host closely before making your choice. Again, your long-range goals for having a blog will come into play.

As was mentioned earlier, LinkedIn has created an interconnection with WordPress (www.WordPress.com); therefore, this is the blogging platform of choice for most LinkedIn members. WordPress offers many perks such as a wide variety of templates, which means you can more nearly match the style of your brand with your blog site graphically. Realize that you don't need the credentials of a programmer to set up a blog. If you can follow directions, you can create a blog site.

## Ready to Build

Now you're ready to build the blog site. Your goal will be to create a leading-edge format that offers information in your niche or area of expertise that will be of interest to others. Use your posts to establish your thoughts and insights in a particular field and exercise your unique voice. Reflect how you have a way of delivering value with your ideas, your input, and your actions.

Be sure your blog bio reflects the profile that you created on LinkedIn. You want to reveal your personality, but in a businesslike manner. For building your brand, you will want to avoid trivia such as your favorite food and most-watched movies.

When creating your actual blog entries, add certain key words. Think of how you want people to find you. When someone is searching for your particular information, what words might be entered into the search engine? The more keywords you use, the better chance you have of ranking high in Google or Yahoo! search engines.

This is known as SEO, or search engine optimization. There are a number of helpful tools that will point you in the right direction as far as which keywords to target in your blog posts. Google AdWords is one such tool. All you do is type in a keyword you're thinking about targeting, and AdWords will tell you not only how popular that search term is, but also how much competition you have for that keyword and even similar keywords that you might consider using as well.

Of course there is much more to SEO than just keywords, but the content is king. Once you've got the content, you can think about hiring a full-service SEO company to really bring your web page to the top of the Google rankings through sophisticated SEO.

Also when creating your blog, keep in mind that your readers are busy people; they don't have time to read a long drawn-out entry. Limit your blogs to around 250 words. And make every word count!

## Interactive

If you think this sounds one-sided, think again. You will set up your blog site to solicit feedback and comments from your readers. In this way you will build new relationships.

Look for other blogs in your related field, visit those sites, and leave your comments. Comments should always add something to the article. Information is essentially free these days, so people no longer feel the need to pay for it. The best way to get your name established as an expert in your field is to pass on free information.

When you comment on someone else's blog with a basic tip or added information about the subject of the blog, you're showing that blogger and her readers that you also have plenty to contribute to the community. Of course it also helps to comment by simply saying something about how great the information is, but that should not be your normal comment. Some incredible network connections can be created by simply sharing information with people who write these blogs. Don't forget to include your name and website on these comments!

An example would go something like this: *Jane, I appreciated your sentiments surrounding organic produce. It was informational and*

*will help me during my next shopping run. Thank you. April Kelly,*
*Author.AprilKelly.com.*

Chances are the author of that blog will reciprocate by
visiting your blog, leave a comment, and possibly subscribe
or follow. Then the readers of that blog may also decide to
subscribe to your blog as well. Soon you will develop your own
community (read that *network*) simply because of your blog.

You can build out your blog by adding multi-media
options such as audios, videos, slideshows, and photos.
Some bloggers seek out experts and invite them to become
"guest'" bloggers on their site. This works to add more
credibility and substance.

Some bloggers add fun games or quizzes to spark more
interest in the site. Use such devices not as a gimmick, but as
a feature that would add to the value of the blog site.

## Blog Maintenance

One of the most prevalent problems with a blog is that it's
relatively easy to start, but blogs can be a challenge to maintain.
If you don't feel you will actually take the time to keep it up,
it's better not to start one at all. Otherwise you might consider
hiring a ghostwriter to handle your blog for you.

There are thousands of competent professionals on
freelance job sites like Elance, Odesk, or Guru. Then you

can simply pass on your topics to your paid ghostwriter and then just make sure that the blog gets posted regularly.

In order to hold your *audience* you will need to post at least two or three times a week. And certainly no less than twice a month. Even that is a bit of a stretch. Regular postings speak volumes about your integrity, your competency, and your ability to follow through.

Now that you have your blog up and running, use the blog URL whenever and wherever you can—in email signatures and on your social network sites, for example. Make sure you are making the best use of your blog site as you continue to build your personal brand and the company called Me, Inc.

Have you ever considered creating your own website? If not, you may reconsider after reading the next chapter.

## 20. Do You Need Your Own Website?

Setting up a blog is fairly simple in that the templates are available and easy to set up and use. While there is a time investment, very little technological expertise is needed. A website is altogether different.

I'm amazed at how few corporate professionals even think about creating their own website. They are content to have their bio and possibly even a photo featured on the corporate site or to be active in a number of social networking sites (usually including LinkedIn). But to have a personalized website seldom occurs to most. Or if the idea does flit by, it is quickly dismissed as something frivolous—just something else to take up valuable time.

The truth is, in today's fast-paced, high-technology-minded world, it's difficult to create a fully rounded-out online presence *without* a personal website. A personal site may showcase the work you are doing with your present employer, but it need not feature that company. Instead the site will place you on center stage. (Me, Inc., remember?) As a tool for brand building, it is one of the most overlooked and least used. Yet it can be one of the strongest tools you have.

## WHERE TO BEGIN

Because you've already designed your own blog, you are halfway home in creating a website. You already have your color scheme, your logo, your domain name, and your theme. And because you did the homework from Part One, you also have your personal brand statement. This statement can be the title of your site.

Begin with site-building software such as Dreamweaver or Expression Web. (These are only two of many that are available.) If you become your own programmer/designer, you will have more control over the finished product and you'll save money as well.

However, if you feel totally lacking in these skills, you can always hire a professional web designer. Keep in mind you may have to pay for setup and maintenance as well, so choose wisely.

Next you need a hosting service. With a paid subscription, these services offer maximum space and can help you get started quickly. Some of the more popular services are 1&1, HostMonster, and GoDaddy. Each has its own advantages. Review them thoroughly before choosing. You might want to ask others who have sites that you admire to tell you their favorite hosting service.

## HAVE FUN!

Building your own site should be a fun experience. It's like facing a large blank artist's canvas. At hand you have a virtual rainbow of colors in your palette and any and all sizes and shapes of brushes. It's your site and your choice as to how you want to be portrayed. Will it be whimsical and light-hearted? Serious and fact-filled? Straightforward and full of power? In all ways this site should reflect your personal brand.

You want your brand statement to be clear and easy to understand, your design to be compelling, and your site to be simple to navigate. The visitor should feel comfortable and interested.

# WHAT TO INCLUDE

What can be included in your site? Here is where your creativity comes into play. What is it you want the reader to know?

A professional photo will play a big part in making the site more personal. A well-written succinct bio will do the same. (This can be the same "about me" bio that you created for your blog.)

- Add your Web links to your social networking sites (more about these sites later) and to your blog. Keep all of these sites interactive.

- List professional skills, experience, career highlights, and endorsements. Sample projects or writing samples can be included as can recent press releases or event notices.

- Pertinent videos will not only supply additional information but will add a powerful element of professionalism. Don't neglect using videos of a speech you made to make your site come alive. One blogger promotes her book by posting home-recorded (but not amateurish) videos of herself reading some of the humorous parts of her book. Did it boost book sales? You bet.

- And don't forget your contact information. At a minimum this should include an email address. You can add a phone number and physical address if it suits your purpose and you are comfortable doing so.

Once your site is up and running, *use it*. Let your URL appear on your résumé, business cards, social networking pages (especially LinkedIn), and signature lines on your emails (if this practice is allowed in your workplace). Keep the invitation open for others to drop by for a visit.

As with a blog, the personal website must be kept up-to-date. As new projects are completed, create a page explaining about the work with added photos or illustrations. The same with awards, promotions, and other professional achievements. Soon you will be coming up with your own original and creative ideas for how to make your site come alive and become memorable to all who visit.

A well-designed, well-maintained website will send the message that this person is dead serious about evoking a strong personal brand. It could be considered almost foolhardy to neglect such a powerful tool.

Having your presence on LinkedIn added to having your own personal blog and website are, in my opinion, the bedrock of brand building. From here let's look at more tools that I consider valid and useful, but optional.

# 21. Social Networking and Still More Online Brand-Building Tools

**B**ecoming involved in social networking sites isn't nearly as powerful as setting up a blog site and a personal website. And in the business and professional arena, they aren't as effective as LinkedIn. That's not to say they cannot be effective.

If the goal is to use social networking sites to advance your career, this will call for careful planning. It can't be used carelessly as you see others doing who are simply chatting with friends and family and looking up old school chums. You must choose a different path and a different method.

Stay with the sites with the largest user base such as Facebook, which is familiar to nearly everyone. This makes your page easier to locate.

Rather than use a cutesy cartoon avatar (small photo) as so many do, you will use the same professional photo that is featured on your blog and website. Here you can also repeat your personal brand statement and add your professional logo.

You will no doubt be able to find groups with like interests to your own—whether in your field of business, hobbies, or charitable endeavors. By joining these and adding comments, you can expand and grow your number of contacts.

Of course for you, the person who is developing and growing your personal brand, this is simply another way to interconnect with your blog, website, and LinkedIn site so that everything neatly fits together.

By this point, you're beginning to see that it's easy to become overloaded and overwhelmed by so many sites to maintain. It will require organization and planning to tend to each of these, but any effort spent will be well rewarded down the road.

Of course just as important as what's on your social networking profile is what's not there. Keep these profiles completely professional so that you would not be ashamed if your employer or potential employers see what's up there. Also many people don't realize the consequences of posting items that are too personal on their networking profile until it is much too late.

For example, a waitress who complained about her customers and named the restaurant she worked for was fired because of the bad reputation she was creating for that restaurant. In fact, many employees who post bad things about the company they work for have been fired.

A mascot for the Pittsburgh Pirates was canned after he made fun of the team's losing streak on his Facebook page. Virgin Airlines fired several flight attendants for disclosing negative information about the company, and an employee at a car dealership in Chicago was fired because he complained about his employer on Facebook. A bartender lost his job because he posted insensitive comments about the patrons of the bar and said that he wished they would "eat glass."

Posting certain pictures of yourself on Facebook also leads to a lot of "negative press" for your personal brand. Photos of you drinking or in various states of undress are not professional and will probably lead to your getting fired or not getting the job you want. A teacher in Georgia was asked to resign when she posted a photo of herself with a drink in each hand while she was on vacation in Europe.

A television meteorologist posted a video of herself doing a risqué dance on her Facebook profile. She is probably one of the few who did not experience immediate backlash at work because of this, but imagine what the viewers of her television station would think if they saw that video. It would be impossible to trust her as an authority on the weather after that. If you were someone considering her for a position, would you hire her? Probably not.

And this concern about photos of you on Facebook extends beyond your own page to the pages of others on Facebook. You can't always control what other people post about you, but you can control the photos they have the opportunity to take. For example, a cheerleader for the New England Patriots was fired after a photo of her apparently drunk and passed out appeared on Facebook. In the photo, you can also see racially insensitive messages and images drawn in pen all over her body.

## ARTICLES

Another way to establish your online identity, strengthen your credibility, and showcase your field of expertise is to write and publish a few articles. You may not be able to get your byline in a big-name trade magazine, but it's relatively simple to publish articles online. There are a myriad of article sites on the Internet, the most well-known of which is EzineArticles.com.

Most professionals in nearly every field have more than enough knowledge to pen a dozen or so short, information-filled articles. The typical length of such articles is from 300 to 700 words.

Some article sites do not allow Web links to be embedded within the article itself. But every site allows the author to create a "resource box" at the end where a short bio and two or more links can be posted. Here is where you can send readers to your blog or website or both.

Once you write and submit an article, there is the possibility of your article being picked up and published by other ezines. As you are finding your voice by creating your brand statement, profile, blog, and website, you can express that same voice in writing articles. In fact, a blog entry could be an article; an article could be a blog entry. There's no reason not to use them interchangeably.

In reviewing all of the online tools that can aid in your brand-building process, article submission is one of the simplest and easiest to implement. And did I mention free?

## PRESS RELEASES

I consider press releases to be a second cousin to writing and publishing online articles. They are just as easy to create; they work to bring attention to your achievements and are free. (Or they *can be* free. Some sites charge a fee.)

When would you use a press release? Any time you make a presentation, win an award, receive a promotion, or are actively involved in a charitable cause, to name just a few.

There are a number of online press-release sites. Their services differ in how extensive their distribution is. This is where the cost comes in: the more extensive the distribution, the more expensive the service. But many that are free can get your name out there and help build your personal brand.

If you're concerned about how to write a good press release, nearly every press release site offers examples to pattern yours. Once you write a few, you'll realize how simple and easy it is. Such little effort for so much reward. Don't leave this tool unused.

# ONLINE RÉSUMÉ

Up to this point, not much has been said about the most basic and most foundational of all tools and that is your résumé. In today's world your résumé will most certainly be online. And as was discussed in the chapters regarding LinkedIn, that site offers a streamlined process for having your résumé online and easily submitted along with a personalized cover letter.

For the most part, a résumé is a résumé is a résumé. And therein lies the problem. What creative (but not gimmicky) way can you make your résumé stand out from the others?

Now that you are confident and comfortable in your personal brand setting, use that as the central theme of your résumé. For those recent college grads, a good deal of your résumé information will pertain to the accomplishments made during your school years.

As you move through a few professional positions, your résumé should reflect that growth. As new listings are added, old ones should drop off. They are no longer pertinent to building your brand. Can you see how the development of your company, Me, Inc., affects everything you do and create?

Outside of having a highly professional and carefully written résumé format, what about including a video? Or possibly descriptive photos showing you involved in charitable work or making a professional presentation. If it's applicable, why not use it?

If résumés are stacking up by the thousands at the online job posting sites and on the desks of human resource professionals around the country, you must take care to have yours command a second look. Since the majority of job seekers are still stuck in the conventional-résumé rut, just a few extra steps on your part can make a world of difference. For example, let's say you have a video clip of a recent presentation you made to a professional group. Include a DVD in your application packet or reference a URL link in your online app.

## MAINTENANCE

In the first chapter of this book I pointed out that people are searching for you on Google whether you like it or not. Because of that fact, it will be necessary that you also Google yourself often. First, you need to see where you are in the rankings, and second, you need to know exactly what is being said about you. There are cases of corporate executives who are shocked to find negative information associated with their names flying around in cyberspace. To be forewarned is to be forearmed, as the old saying goes.

If this ever happens to you, your attention to your Web identity can prevent extensive damage. Keep in mind how fast information and opinions can travel on the Internet. If you're on top of your online presence, negative information can be squelched before it gets out of hand. You don't want it to be a hiring manager who is performing a Google search on your name to discover your bad press.

If and when you do discover a negative comment or opinion in connection with your name and your personal brand, you need to go into recovery mode. If it occurs on someone's blog, you can counter with a comment of your own on that blog clarifying the issue. You can add a blog on your own site that states your side of the issue. Or you may even want to privately email that blogger in an attempt to make things right. In so doing, there's a chance you could even make a friend.

Because Google PageRank results are based on ever-changing algorithms, the power to change the rankings is in your hands. (*PageRank* refers to a link analysis algorithm, named after Larry *Page*, used by the Google Internet search engine.) By learning the techniques, you can set about building more and more positive listings, which will then push the negative ones down. The result will be that your bad press is buried and will be seen by fewer and fewer online visitors.

One of the benefits of a blog site is that it offers "page freshness" to your Google rankings. As you continually update your blog, it is again indexed by search engines and drives up your rankings.

Understanding SEO (search engine optimization) also aids in boosting rankings. SEO is based mainly on keywords: how many occur, where they appear, and how frequently they appear within one page. SEO experts know to place the most keywords near the top of the Web page and place them as close together as possible, while maintaining the clarity of the message. Place your keywords in phrases that someone browsing for your information might search for.

The study of SEO is too broad and extensive to present in this book, but it's good to have a basic understanding as you build your online brand identity and cultivate your Google presence.

Another key to higher rankings is the links system. Invest the time to interlink with many other sites. This means that you add a hotlink to another URL on your website in exchange for someone else adding yours to their site. It's an exchange of links to increase traffic to both. By receiving a link from another site that enjoys a high PageRank, your rankings will soar. Locate like-minded individuals who perhaps are in your same industry and suggest to them that you exchange links. Everyone benefits from such exchanges.

Even if there is no exchange, you can still link to other sites if you feel it reinforces a point or makes an illustration for your blog. Either way, it's a simple, quick, and easy way to push your sites—and your name—higher on the Google search pages.

Internal linking within your own blog or website will also enhance rankings. For instance, to make a point in a blog, link to one of your earlier blogs that is closely related.

I've already pointed out the incredible benefits of membership on LinkedIn, and one of those benefits is the way in which it boosts Google PageRank. Sites like

LinkedIn, Twitter, Facebook, YouTube, and others carry a lot of weight on Google.

A full understanding of all these online techniques will aid you in achieving the PageRank that you need to showcase your brand and to drive down and make invisible any negative press you may have received. Ignorance and negligence can be deadly on the Internet. It pays to be proactive.

Building your personal brand will forever be a work in progress. You will do well to treat it as such.

No matter how vast and how effective the Internet may be, there is still a physical world to consider, and your brand building will spill over into this world as well.

## 22. Brand-Building Offline

If you look great on your website, write knock-em-dead blogs and articles, yet fail miserably when in the workplace interacting with real, live people, such inconsistency can prove disastrous. When building your personal brand, every part must join with and support the other parts in order to make the whole.

## WHAT ABOUT THE OFFICE?

Your personality, your demeanor, your attitude and even how you present yourself physically (appearance) are all vital in rounding out Me, Inc. If someone were to walk into your office area and you were not there, what impression would that person make just from glancing around? Are there mounds of clutter and papers scattered here and there? Or are things neat and tidy? Have you considered ways in which the theme of your brand might be reflected on your office walls, or on your desk?

If you thought your office appearance wasn't important, now it very much is. Because, like it or not, your office is part and parcel of your personal brand.

## WHAT ABOUT PERSONAL APPEARANCE?

The trend in recent years toward a more laid-back dress code in the office is not an excuse for sloppiness. A professional look is still respected and appreciated. The term *business casual* seems to be everywhere. This still means showing up in pants that are pressed and a shirt with a collar. You don't want to take anything for granted when you are working in a casual environment. When in doubt, dress up or beyond the code.

In addition to promoting your image, a professional look also enhances the level of a person's confidence. It's a proven fact that people who feel good about how they look exude a vibrancy and a higher level of enthusiasm.

What you wear, how you converse, and your body language all speak a language that describes exactly who you are. And each one is yet another tool to be used in the brand-building process. Carefully consider each one and take care how they can work for you.

## WHAT ABOUT THE SMALL THINGS?

When you think of FedEx, what color comes to mind? Yes, purple. How about UPS? Again, a color (brown) has been built around the UPS brand. Same with Home Depot's orange and red for Target. Giant corporations seldom leave color to chance. Neither should you.

Think about color that you can use that will add strong statements into your brand. This can be carried out in areas of dress (suits, ties), accessories (shoes, purses, jewelry), and in your office décor (art, upholstery, wall colors).

If it works for the big fish, it can work for you.

Don't overlook small items such as business cards. Even though you may have corporate business cards, there's no reason why you cannot also print your own personalized cards that reflect your brand and highlight your logo, your blog, and your website. Matching personalized stationery and note cards can do the same thing.

# EVENTS AND OUTSIDE ACTIVITIES

Because you did the work in the opening chapters of this book, you have tapped into your passion and have an understanding of what it is that makes you feel life is worth living. If it doesn't appear that you can use those passions in your workplace, look for outside avenues such as professional organizations or charitable causes.

Become involved in events such as industry conventions, career fairs, workshops, or civic activities. The key is to make sure what you choose fits with the direction you want your life and your future to take. Avoid involvement solely for the sake of involvement, which becomes totally counter-productive.

Just as a large company works hard to manage its brand, you must likewise manage your personal brand in every area of your life. Living your brand is the subject of the next chapter.

# 23. Impressions and Reputations

When it comes to personal branding, you are essentially trying to control what others think of you. You're establishing a professional identity that not only shows who you are, but does it in such a way that you will be remembered in a positive way by others. The basis of personal branding involves impression and reputation management, in addition to making the most of your reputation capital.

## IMPRESSION: WHAT OTHERS THINK OF YOU

Impression management requires you to make certain goals to create a process that will influence what others think about you in a very positive way. You can do this by controlling your social interactions with others. To see how real professionals control the impressions of the public and what society thinks of them, their company, and their product, let's take a look at how public relations firms and the PR departments of major corporations function.

PR is a term companies throw around all the time, but what does it really mean? It's about promoting the image of the company in a positive way and avoiding anything that detracts from what society thinks of that company. PR is also about managing various communications among businesses and society.

Public relations is built around preserving the image of the company and influencing society to think positively about the company. This brings about positive rewards for the company, which generally results in higher sales because the average consumer thinks highly of the company's brand.

For individuals, there are many more components of impression management to deal with. You do want to influence others to think well of you, but the way you paint yourself can fall along several lines. For example, you might try to put on your best face all the time so that others will like you. This is a great technique for personal branding in some respects, but it may not always be appropriate. Some companies are not looking for a woman or a man who seems to be too easy on her employees.

On the other hand, some men and women go for the intimidation image, in which their anger comes quickly and easily as a way to get others to do what they say. Some women, in particular, fall into a third category when it comes to impression management, and that involves making herself appear vulnerable so that others feel the need to help her constantly.

The best bet for personal branding is to fall somewhere in the middle of the first two. The third category won't get you to the top of anywhere. It may work as a method for getting others to do your work for you, but that impression will catch up with you after a short time. Some women find themselves in that category without the knowledge of how to undo that impression.

Generally there are two ways around it. You could simply put a stop to the manipulation tactics and start doing your own work. This is an uphill battle that's worth it if you want to change the way your career is going. However it will take time and a lot of damage control on your part. If you can manage to snag a similar position at a different company, you have the opportunity to begin fresh and start building a better impression of yourself with your coworkers.

Let's go back to looking at the first two categories of impressions. No matter what kind of position you are seeking, it's important to make sure that you are seen as a great person to work for and with, but also as someone who is no pushover. Impression management is important because whenever you're interviewing for a job—and especially when you're going for a big-time corporate position—you will be under scrutiny. Even if right now you're not looking for a position, you should manage others' impressions of you as if you are currently being scrutinized. If you don't, the impressions you build right now could come back to haunt you later.

The key to building good impressions is to examine your behavior in corporate and social settings. It may seem a little off-putting to imagine someone always watching what you do, but that's how impression management works. You're trying to build up positive impressions so that others see you as someone who will provide great value to their company.

Some companies operate on the belief that there is no such thing as bad publicity because any publicity (good or bad) is publicity, but this could not be further from the truth when you're talking about personal branding. Sometimes creating a buzz around a product may involve taking a few hits along the way just to get people talking about it, but this is certainly no way to build your personal brand. Getting people to know who you are only has a positive outcome if the perspective they have of you is positive as well.

## REPUTATION: WHAT OTHERS SAY ABOUT YOU

Reputation management is related to impression management, but it is slightly different. For example, reputation management usually relates to individuals rather than businesses, although businesses can also track their reputation.

There are thousands of private firms that offer professional reputation management, which involves tracking and reporting on what they learn about your reputation, usually online. Another option would be to purchase and use online reputation management software. However, it is not usually necessary to go to such extremes to analyze your reputation. Most of the time you can go by what people are saying about you.

For example, if you were a fly on the wall of an office in which two people were discussing you, what would they be saying? It is both easier and more difficult to discover this information than to analyze the data that's out there online. Some individuals hire private firms so they can find out what others are saying about them. However, having a dream team of individuals in place works just the same way. It's easier to find out what others are saying about you by enlisting the help of people you trust to find out this information about you.

Just remember that the goal is not to engage in back-stabbing, gossipy behavior. It's about finding out what kind of reputation you have in a unique way that allows you to work on that reputation.

The other aspect of reputation management is the opportunity to respond to what others say about you. This may involve subtle responses such as changed behavior when you hear what others are saying about you or more direct responses in the form of online responses that are posted to feedback written about you.

Reputation capital is also important in the world of personal branding, but the concept can be a little more difficult to grasp than the other two mentioned in this chapter. Reputation capital is actually the measure of your reputation within your community or marketplace.

Studies have shown, for example, that users with a negative rating of just 1 percent can actually anticipate a lower price for their item. The negative rating will cost you an average of 4 percent on a sale. Just a few points can mean the difference between landing that job or not landing it. Making a sale or not making it. Reputation capital is probably one of the most important aspects of personal branding and also one of the least understood.

The issue many people have is that, in many cases, reputation capital seems like it is something that can't be measured. However, it can be measured most of the time; you just have to know where to look in order to discover the measurements you are looking for.

If you're blogging regularly, the best place to look is Google PageRank. This measures the popularity of your blog. The popularity measure of your blog is one indication of your reputation capital. Technorati, a search engine specifically used to search blogs, has an authority rating for each of the blogs it indexes. Looking at this rating is another way to measure your reputation capital.

It is imperative that you manage your online reputation. You can play a large role in your reputation through various tools such as blogs and a personal website. You can further enhance your brand through what others say about you.

Online brand management has evolved to the point where there are even online services that will monitor your online data and help you minimize negative content. The best way to do this is through monitoring activity that includes your name and developing a reputation for good content, good service, good work, or whatever your vocation.

Remember, an incident that happens right now will be tweeted about online before you can even begin dialing your phone. If the comment is positive, you'll get a huge boost to your brand and reputation.

## 24. Living Your Personal Brand

There's probably nothing more miserable than an unfocused, directionless life. Everything becomes monotonous and dreary. Days are brim-full of the mundane, and the next day is more of the same. The highest goal is to "get through the day." Or "hang on til Friday."

The unfocused, directionless life smacks of feeling trapped. Unable to move. It's a reactive life where things happen "to" you as opposed to you making things happen. This is very much a "herd" mentality. It stands to reason that herds are "herded" and are seldom in control.

You Can Do It!

# OUT OF THE PIT,
## ONTO THE HIGH ROAD

I've seen the concepts of personal branding through networking bring despondent, directionless people out of the pit of trapped feelings and put them on a high road to greater success and greater self-satisfaction.

I've seen the concepts of personal branding through networking take a highly talented individual who was stagnating in a dead-end job and lift her to a place where her talents could shine. Where her distinct personality could stand out from the crowd and where she could fulfill her highest goals in life.

Why? What makes the discovery of personal branding so powerful? The answer to that is many things, but the chief aspect is that personal branding is within your grasp. It doesn't matter where you are in your career, developing your personal brand puts you in the driver's seat. It puts you at the helm of Me, Inc. Such empowerment can equip you to become all you dreamed you wanted to be. And anyone can do it!

Social media is within the reach of all. Social media has transcended all of the old, in-the-past traditional communication channels. You don't have to be a rock star or ace athlete and pay big bucks to a crack public relations firm to get your name out there. The power is in your hands. You can do it yourself. (With the help of your network, of course.)

Take advantage of all the amazing tools that are available today. Tools that even a decade ago were not readily available. But what good are tools if they are not used?

The only thing that stands between you and your having a distinctive, memorable personal brand is your decision to begin. And the only thing that hinders the step to begin is not knowing —

- Who you are,
- What you want, and
- Where you are going.

And that takes us back to the first chapters. Personal branding truly does begin with you putting yourself at the helm of Me, Inc. You must respect your*self* enough to take these needed steps. Find out who you are and dig deep to discover your true passions. (If you have buried them, this may take time.) You can never build your personal brand if you are afraid to be *yourself!*

Building your personal brand, creating Me, Inc., will not happen in a day. It will require time, attention, diligence, and organization. (Often spelled w-o-r-k.) However, as I have pointed out, there is a point of critical mass where all of your diligence and hard work will begin to pay off in exponential results. Your sphere of influence will spread out in ever-widening, concentric circles affecting greater numbers of people. Your individuality will be recognized; your efforts will garner respect. You will have a more fulfilled life. Those rewards will be worth it all.

# LIVE TO GIVE

Another word of advice is to enter into brand building with a giving attitude. Always be on the lookout as to how you can be of benefit to others around you. Look for opportunities to reach out and lend a hand. Be as ready to give introductions and recommendations on LinkedIn as you are to receive them. Look for opportunities on the job to give an encouraging word and to go the extra mile. Look for opportunities in your community to give back at every turn. Investing in others is one of the best ways to build your personal brand. It's a principle that never fails.

## Gratitude

My first book, *Gratitude at Work: How to Say Thank You, Give Kudos, and Get the Best from Those You Lead,* talks extensively about the "magic" of having an attitude of gratitude. Throughout my career, I've learned that a simple, yet sincere, *thank you* can go a long way in helping to create your identity—both online and offline.

Never fail to look for opportunities to extend a word of thanks, or a note of thanks, or a way to offer an unexpected gift to someone within your realm of influence. It's my heartfelt belief that fostering gratitude is effective in all business relationships, but especially in the leadership role.

What better way to reinforce your unique personal brand than to be a person who is known as someone who is appreciative and thankful in all situations—both good and bad? Place gratitude near the top of your list of attributes and live it on a daily basis, and watch your success grow exponentially.

That's it! You've thrown a lot of *Spaghetti on the Wall.* What's sticking?

You are now fully aware of the value and necessity of developing your own personal brand in this day and age. This is a book to be kept close at hand—used more as a reference than one for casual reading. As you walk through your brand-building journey, you will want to refer to it often.

# Final Course

In the early days of the Internet, those who had millions of dollars to throw at this new phenomenon seemed to be sorely lacking in foresight.

They spent unbelievable amounts of money to purchase ho-hum, lackluster, plain-Jane, going-nowhere domain names. Look at these figures:

Business.com was bought for $7.5 million

Wine.com was bought for $3 million

Telephone.com was bought for $1.75 million

Bingo.com was bought for $1.1 million

Wallstreet.com was bought for $1.03 million

Drugs.com was bought for $823,456

University.com was bought for $530,000[1]

It is any wonder there was a dot com bust? Do you think any of those people ever made their investments back? Highly unlikely.

Those with the clever, outstanding, memorable names like Yahoo!, amazon, eBay, and PayPal came along later!

In the very same way, those individuals today who are sorely lacking in foresight with regard to their careers will be doomed to the same fate. For those who continue to use outdated, ho-hum, lackluster, plain-Jane, going-nowhere résumés and cover letters, the future is sure to be dim indeed. One would have to wonder why any professional would opt to settle for such dead-end avenues when so much is at stake—and when so many other choices are now available.

Every tool is in place to enable you to manage your own career in a Web 2.0 world. Why blend in with the woodwork and hide in the shadows when you have every opportunity to unearth and embrace your own particular individuality? (Also remember that employers are now expecting their professionals to self-market and are looking for the same!)

While the power to manage your career and shape your personal brand is within your grasp, that power is useless if not implemented. No one will care more about Me, Inc., than you. And no one will give it more love and attention than you. No one knows better how to showcase your talents, gifts, and abilities than you.

Your network is a commodity; your network is your goodwill ambassador. Make a quality decision to let networking be an ongoing daily process in your life. Take full responsibility to make that network work for you in the growth of your brand and your future career. Your personal brand will become the platform from which you will stand up and say to the world: "Here I am!"

[1] Al Ries and Laura Ries, *The 22 Immutable Laws of Branding*, Collins Business, 2002.

# About the Author

April Kelly was working for PayPal before they were PayPal, laying the foundation and building the company from the ground up.

In her next role, as the senior director of customer operations at LinkedIn, she would be placed in the center of another dot com revolution: professional networking. She started, staffed, and unlocked the door to the customer service center for LinkedIn in Omaha in late 2006. Today, the office supports over 100 million LinkedIn users worldwide.

April is a firm believer in networking to build a personal brand. As with her first book, *Gratitude at Work: How to Say Thank You, Give Kudos, and Get the Best from Those You Lead* (also from WooHoo Press at AuthorAprilKelly.com), she practices what she preaches. Her professional life is supported and has advanced by quality networking. And her personal brand makes a strong statement about her and her contributions to the workplace and to the community at large.

## Resources for April Kelly:

Follow April's latest muse at her blog site:
GratitudeAtWork.wordpress.com

Visit her website:
AuthorAprilKelly.com.

Her acrylic artwork can be seen at one of these galleries:
Springfield Artworks (SpringfieldArtworks.com)
or Seven Arrows Gallery (7ArrowsGallery.com)

Her Professional Guide is available here:
LinkedIn.com/in/AprilKelly